Basic Financial Accounting Theory

R. F. SALMONSON

Michigan State University

WADSWORTH PUBLISHING COMPANY, INC.
BELMONT, CALIFORNIA

L. C. Cat. Card No.: 69-14213

Printed in the United States of America

PREFACE

For far too many years, financial accounting has been taught at the undergraduate collegiate level primarily with emphasis upon the mechanics of problem solving. Because inadequate attention is devoted to the framework of accounting thought, the undergraduate accounting major at graduation is virtually a theory illiterate, viewing accounting theory as the mass of unintegrated rules he has memorized.

This book was written to aid in correcting this impression. It is, therefore, designed primarily for use at the senior level. But, because the most essential prerequisite is the completion of intermediate accounting, it can be used near the end of the second year of accounting study. It can also be used at the graduate level for those whose undergraduate accounting education did not include a course in accounting theory. Graduate students without prior accounting education who have completed at least one year of accounting study should be able to use the book successfully. Study of this book should also prove useful for those planning to write the theory section of the Uniform CPA Examination.

The book contains six chapters. The first chapter discusses the various approaches employed in erecting a structure of accounting theory and the attributes and uses of theory. Chapter 2 illustrates the eclectic nature of accounting theory by presenting the historical development of a number of the ideas currently considered fundamental to accounting. The question is raised about whether, in view of the diverse origins of these ideas, accounting objectives might not be conflicting. Chapter 3 presents and contrasts the basic accounting concepts contained in an inventory of accounting principles with the postulates considered basic to several deductive models of accounting theory.

Because the determination of periodic net income is still the financial accountant's major task, two chapters deal with the nature and measurement of income. Chapter 4 contains a discussion of the psychological, economic, and accounting concepts of income.

Chapter 5 explores the accountant's concept of income more fully by delving into the questions of revenue and expense recognition. Here the theme is that no real comprehension of accounting theory is possible until it is fully recognized how completely the determination of periodic net income dominates both accounting theory and practice.

Contrasted briefly in Chapter 6 are a normative set of accounting principles and an inventory of current generally accepted accounting principles. Because of the existence of a vast array of accepted alternatives, financial information may differ substantially among entities solely because of the accounting alternatives employed. Chapter 6, after detailing some of these alternatives, concludes with a discussion of the extent to which the accounting undertaken can and should be uniform to secure the desired comparability in financial information.

A number of questions are presented at the end of each chapter for review and discussion purposes. Many of the ideas presented in this book are footnoted not only to indicate their source but to provide the student with references for further study—formally directed or independent. In this regard, the author wishes to express his appreciation to the American Institute of Certified Public Accountants for permission to quote at length from several of its publications.

The author wishes to acknowledge his indebtedness and to express his appreciation to many for their assistance in bringing this book to publication—to Dr. Robert H. Gregory, and to Dr. A. N. Mosich of the University of Southern California for many valuable comments and criticisms of the entire manuscript; to Dr. Stephen A. Zeff of Tulane University for valuable criticisms of an earlier draft; to many graduate students for comments on parts of this and prior drafts; and to Merrilyn Vaughn for the quick and accurate typing services rendered. A special, indirect debt is owed to Dr. William A. Paton of the University of Michigan, whose teachings, writings, and personal friendship have been a constant source of inspiration and encouragement. But, perhaps, the greatest debt is owed to my wife, Jo, for simply putting up with me while this book was being written.

CONTENTS

1. THE NATURE, USES, AND ATTRIBUTES OF ACCOUNTING THEORY *1*

   Accounting Theory Defined *1*
   The Practical Approach *2*
      The Practical Approach Illustrated *3*
      Advantages of the Practical Approach *3*
      Disadvantages of the Practical Approach *4*
   The Deductive Approach *5*
      The Deductive Approach Illustrated *6*
      Advantages of the Deductive Approach *7*
      Disadvantages of the Deductive Approach *7*
   The Inductive Approach *8*
      The Inductive Approach Illustrated *8*
      Advantages of the Inductive Approach *9*
      Disadvantages of the Inductive Approach *9*
   The Ethical Approach *10*
      The Ethical Approach Illustrated *10*
      Advantages of the Ethical Approach *11*
      Disadvantages of the Ethical Approach *11*
   Other Approaches and Views *12*
   Accounting Theory in the Future *14*
   The Uses of Theory *14*
      Nondirective Uses *14*
      Directive Uses *15*
   The Attributes of Accounting Theory *16*
   Summary *17*

2. THE SOURCES OF ACCOUNTING THEORY   *20*

Environmental Influences   *20*
  Double-Entry Bookkeeping   *20*
  Continuity of Business Activity   *21*
  The Influence of the Corporation   *23*
  Influence of Taxation   *25*
  Influence of Economic Theory   *27*
  Influence of the Regulation of
    Public Utilities and Railroads   *28*
  Influence of Economic and Social Conditions   *29*
Organizational Influences   *32*
  American Institute of Certified Public
    Accountants   *32*
  The American Accounting Association   *36*
  Securities Legislation and the Securities and
    Exchange Commission   *39*
A Concluding Observation   *43*

3. THE BASIC CONCEPTS   *46*

The Nature of Basic Concepts   *47*
A Society and Government Structure Honoring
  Private-Property Rights   *48*
Specific Business Entities   *49*
Going Concern (Continuity)   *51*
Monetary Expression in Accounts   *53*
Consistency between Periods for the Same Entity   *55*
Diversity in Accounting among Independent Entities   *56*
Conservatism   *57*
Dependability of Data through Internal Control   *58*
Materiality   *61*
Timeliness in Financial Reporting Requires Estimates   *63*
Comparative Summary   *64*

4. INCOME CONCEPTS   *69*

    Psychic Income   *70*
    Economic Income   *70*
      Capitalized Net Receipts   *71*
    Market Values   *74*
    Accounting Income   *75*
      The Transactions Approach   *76*
      Accounting Income and Changing Price Levels   *78*
      Current Cost   *88*
      Income Inclusions and Exclusions   *90*
    Summary   *94*

5. REVENUES AND EXPENSES   *97*

    Revenue Recognition   *97*
      Revenue Defined   *98*
      Revenue Measurement   *99*
      The Time of Revenue Recognition   *100*
      Bases of Revenue Recognition   *105*
      Summary of Revenue Recognition   *108*
    Expense Recognition   *109*
      Expense Defined   *109*
      Expense Measurement   *111*
      The Time of Expense Recognition   *114*
      Summary of Expense Recognition   *118*

6. PRINCIPLES, ALTERNATIVES, AND
   UNIFORMITY   *123*

      Accounting Research Study No. 3   *123*
      Accounting Research Study No. 7   *125*
      Alternatives in Accounting   *131*
      Effects of Alternatives   *134*

The Uniformity-Diversity Controversy   *136*
The Real Issues   *137*
Semantic Problems   *139*
The Need to State Objectives   *140*
Disagreement on Approach   *141*
Lack of Knowledge of Economic Flows   *144*
Comparability and Relevance   *146*
Summary   *146*

INDEX   *150*

1

THE NATURE, USES, AND ATTRIBUTES OF ACCOUNTING THEORY

To study the theory of a field of knowledge is to inquire into its fundamental nature, to deal with its substance rather than its form, to focus upon essential concepts, notions, or natural laws rather than upon their application. And real comprehension may be obtainable only from a study of theory since practices are often incomplete and not necessarily logical expressions of theory.

This chapter presents a definition of accounting theory, explores and illustrates some of the approaches to building a structure of theory, indicates the need for theory, and cites the attributes it must possess to be useful.

ACCOUNTING THEORY DEFINED

Accounting theory consists of a cohesive set of conceptual, hypothetical, and pragmatic propositions "explaining and guiding the accountant's action in identifying, measuring, and communicating economic information." [1] The term "proposition" is defined as any declarative statement, true or false. It is used to include in the body of theory ideas not universally acceptable, but advanced for explanation or for guidance of practice.

Although we say "accounting theory" there are actually many

[1]Committee to Prepare a Statement of Basic Accounting Theory, *A Statement of Basic Accounting Theory* (Evanston, Ill.: American Accounting Association, 1966), pp. 1–2.

theories of accounting currently espoused—none fully organized into a single, logical structure of thought.[2]

THE PRACTICAL APPROACH

To the majority of accountants today, accounting is a utilitarian art.[3] The American Institute of Certified Public Accountants concurs in this view, as implied from the approach in its accounting research bulletins published from 1939 to 1959.[4] For the most part, these bulletins provided immediate practical solutions to pressing problems, without concern for internal consistency among all solutions recommended. Under this approach, theory is largely rational justification and explanation of practice.[5] The approach is similar to setting speed limits on streets and highways by observing the speed at which traffic moves. The heavy reliance upon practice often leads to the assertion, "If it's not good practice, it's not good theory."

A generally accepted principle evolves out of practice somewhat along the following lines. For any of a variety of reasons—war versus peace, inflation versus depression—a problem in providing useful information is encountered. After careful consideration, a certain practice is formulated as a solution. The solution may meet ready acceptance, or it may require modification, or it may even be rejected. In any event, a particular practice becomes acceptable to many, if not to all. Thus is developed a general rule or guide to accounting action which is, under the practical approach,

---

[2]For an extended discussion, see Eldon S. Hendriksen, *Accounting Theory* (Homewood, Ill.: Richard D. Irwin, Inc., 1965), pp. 1–13. Also see Harvey T. Deinzer, *Development of Accounting Thought* (New York: Holt, Rinehart and Winston, Inc., 1965), esp. Chap. 4, and John W. Buckley, Paul Kircher, and Russell L. Mathews, "Methodology in Accounting Theory," *The Accounting Review,* Vol. 43 (April 1968), pp. 274–283.

[3]William W. Werntz, "The Influence of Administrative Agencies on Accounting," in *Handbook of Modern Accounting Theory,* Morton Backer, ed. (New York: Prentice-Hall, Inc., 1953), p. 18. See also Robert E. Witschey, "Accounting Theory and the Accounting Profession," in *Modern Accounting Theory,* Morton Backer, ed. (Englewood Cliffs, N. J.: Prentice-Hall, Inc., 1966), p. 2, and T. K. Cowan, "A Pragmatic Approach to Accounting Theory," *The Accounting Review,* Vol. 43 (January 1968), p. 94.

[4]Committees on Accounting Procedure and Terminology, *Accounting Research and Terminology Bulletins,* Final Edition (New York: American Institute of Certified Public Accountants, 1961).

[5]A. C. Littleton and V. K. Zimmerman, *Accounting Theory: Continuity and Change* (Englewood Cliffs, N. J.: Prentice-Hall, Inc., 1962), pp. 10, 128ff.

a principle of accounting. It rests upon satisfactory experience, legal requirements, and contractual arrangements, not upon formal and internally consistent reasoning processes.[6]

Definitions and working rules are established to implement the principles. These principles, definitions, and rules, together with explanation and justification, constitute the body of theory under the practical approach. Their evolution out of successful practice explains why the notions of materiality, objectivity, consistency, disclosure, and conservatism are often referred to as principles of accounting.

The Practical Approach Illustrated

According to Vance, the pricing of inventories at the lower of cost or market dates back to Italy in the early 1400s.[7] The reasons why it was employed at that time are not known. The method gained further acceptance in England in the mid-1800s and was widely used in the United States in the early 1900s because its application resulted in a conservative balance sheet.[8] Such conservatism was viewed favorably by bankers and other lenders, who were then the primary users of balance sheets. Since then, cost or market has been tied to other accounting methods. But of all methods of inventory measurement, none is criticized more for its lack of consistency and logic.[9] And this criticism is not of recent origin.[10] Yet it is still used, simply because it is believed that valuable and conservative information results.

Advantages of the Practical Approach

The accounting function is valuable to society only if it provides useful information. In the practical approach, the primary requirement is that the application of a theoretical proposition must provide useful information. Ideas from many sources will be accepted if proven useful.

[6]Paul Grady, "Inventory of Generally Accepted Accounting Principles for Business Enterprises," *Accounting Research Study No. 7* (New York: American Institute of Certified Public Accountants, 1965), p. 55.

[7]Lawrence L. Vance, "The Authority of History in Inventory Valuation," *The Accounting Review,* Vol. 28 (July 1943), p. 219.

[8]Littleton and Zimmerman, *op.cit.,* pp. 154–155.

[9]For a discussion in depth, see W. A. Paton and W. A. Paton, Jr., *Asset Accounting* (New York: The Macmillan Company, 1952), pp. 75–88.

[10]Littleton and Zimmerman, *op. cit.,* p. 155.

The practical approach is based upon the assumption that the practitioner knows what is useful. If this is true, the practices developed will be optimal—that is, they will provide the best information possible, considering the practical difficulties of accumulating it. If there is general agreement that certain practices can be applied and that their application will provide useful information, some degree of uniformity of practice may follow. And with emphasis upon tried and proven ideas, theory is not cluttered with ideas that cannot be implemented.

Disadvantages of the Practical Approach

The main disadvantage of this approach is that a completely unstructured body of propositions results, primarily because there is no clear statement of objectives. Useful information is to be provided—but useful to whom and for what? The propositions included are undoubtedly useful but not necessarily for attaining the same objective. Some are useful in delaying income tax payments, or in enhancing reported net income, or in meeting regulatory requirements, while others are adopted because they are easily implemented. Some of the propositions may actually be inconsistent, thus raising questions about which should be followed. For example, the immediate expensing of the costs of promoting a new product may be a logical move to delay the payment of income taxes. But will such a practice yield information useful to help stockholders in appraising their investments? The formulation of a theory of accounting without an explicit statement of objectives seems impossible.

Another serious deficiency is the lack of a mechanism to remove outmoded propositions. The usual approach is simply to add new propositions.[11] Thus, theory is burdened with ever increasing numbers of propositions which possess varying degrees of acceptance and which often produce vastly different results. Since, under this approach, theory is largely the rationalization of practice, the body of theory must contain some propositions which are in conflict.

Storey has pointed out that the pragmatic approach has seldom produced lasting solutions to problems since the American Institute and its committees have found themselves continually dealing

---

[11]Reed K. Storey, *The Search for Accounting Principles* (New York: American Institute of Certified Public Accountants, 1964), p. 49.

with the same problem. The recent experience with pension accounting is an example. And further, some solutions presented have created other problems which the practical approach has not been able to solve.[12] For example, the solution to the appraisal problem — that accounting be based on historical cost — has created the unsolved problem of how to proceed when general or specific price levels change substantially.

Because the practical approach emphasizes the use of theory to justify and explain practice, it would appear that theory can only follow practice. But it would be unfair to state that according to this approach accountants act instinctively when faced with a problem and then seek rational justification for their actions. Certainly reasoning plays a part in determining what action is to be taken; the reasoning is simply not formally structured or explicitly stated.

THE DEDUCTIVE APPROACH

The basic elements of the deductive approach to the formulation of accounting theory are (1) objectives, (2) postulates, (3) principles, and (4) rules. The *objectives* must be clearly stated to provide guidance in completing the model. The *postulates* describe the economic, political, and sociological environment in which accounting must function. They are based on observation and are stated in primitives which are believed to be so readily understood that they avoid circular reasoning. The following terms are examples of primitives in accounting: exchange, property, claim, transaction, and equity.[13]

Propositions are then advanced, together with necessary definitions, stating how the objectives sought are to be achieved within the given environment. These propositions are developed through reasoning, and if it can be shown that they do follow logically and their application leads to the attainment of objectives, they are called *principles*. Some principles are descriptive or classificational; others are normative. Normative principles — those which state what ought to be — include legal, moral, and professional standards.[14]

---

[12]*Ibid.,* p. 52.

[13]Eric L. Kohler, *A Dictionary for Accountants,* Third Edition (Englewood Cliffs, N. J.: Prentice-Hall, Inc., 1963), pp. 394–395.

[14]*Ibid.,* p. 395.

For example, the fiction in law of the prudent man is a normative principle.

Rules are then added as specific directives to action to achieve the results indicated by the principles. In its abstract form the structure of theory then consists of objectives, postulates, principles, definitions, rules, and the reasoning binding them together into a logical, coherent, consistent model.

But in order to apply the model in accounting a basic structure is needed. In the past, this has been the double-entry system of recording with its accounts, ledgers, journals, and the resulting financial statements. But it need not take only these forms. All that is required is an input-output mechanism to receive and process the raw data into the desired information.

There are constraints to developing principles to bridge objectives and postulates. These constraints, inherent in the accounting environment, relate primarily to the uncertainty that surrounds accounting measurements because they are based upon expectations and because of changes in the value of money.[15] Objectivity, tentativeness, and consistency are constraints; they will be discussed in a later chapter.

The Deductive Approach Illustrated

In the production of goods and services for exchange in our society, certain entities employ resources (assets, wealth) supplied by others. For decision making, those supplying the resources need information, such as the amount of resources held by a specific entity. An objective of accounting is to supply such information. (Note how closely postulates and objectives are related. The objectives of accounting are kept in mind when the environment is observed while formulating basic postulates.)

A principle of accounting logically follows. All assets owned, regardless of source, should be recorded and reported in the financial statements in order to provide information on the amount of assets owned by an entity.[16]

Acceptance of the traditional framework of the accounting system is indicated through use of accounts for accumulating data

---

[15]Hendriksen, *op. cit.,* p. 4.

[16]This is a principle in the deductive approach as advocated in Robert T. Sprouse and Maurice Moonitz, "A Tentative Set of Broad Accounting Principles for Business Enterprises," *Accounting Research Study No. 3* (New York: American Institute of Certified Public Accountants, 1962), p. 55.

and financial statements for reporting them. But difficulties are encountered in applying the above principle. The intangible assets of an accounting unit simply cannot always be measured with precision. The basic principle is modified somewhat in its application so that it now directs the recording and reporting of all assets verifiably measurable.

Advantages of the Deductive Approach

The advantages of the deductive approach include the formulation of a complete, coordinated, consistent structure of theory with each step following logically from its predecessor. Internal consistency between propositions is attained. Orderliness of thought and method characterize the deductive approach, rather than the seeming haphazardness of the practical approach.

Furthermore, each principle is carefully examined for its logic and to determine whether its application will help attain known objectives. And the model's normative propositions can serve as standards in the evaluation of various accounting practices.

Disadvantages of the Deductive Approach

The deductive model is founded upon postulates and assumed objectives which may be proven false. If so, the derived principles may also be false. A logical structure of theory cannot consist of false premises and principles.

Many postulates describing our society could be formulated, and the deductive approach does not contain the needed selection criteria for determining those applicable to accounting. The boundaries of the accounting discipline may be unduly limited if the approach is to "explore as much of the environment as relates to the problems that accountants deal with." [17] The possibility of overlooking some problems should be obvious.

The deductive approach is often criticized for yielding accounting principles which are "theoretical hypotheses untried in practice or tried and discarded as impractical." [18] The implication is that the approach does not rely heavily enough upon experience. But

---

[17]Maurice Moonitz, "The Basic Postulates of Accounting," *Accounting Research Study No. 1* (New York: American Institute of Certified Public Accountants, 1961), p. 5.

[18]"Comments of Carman G. Blough," in Robert T. Sprouse and Maurice Moonitz, *op. cit.*, p. 60.

such a view unduly restricts theory by tying it too closely to what is practical and capable of implementation, and it denies the use of theory in formulating new ideas or principles.

THE INDUCTIVE APPROACH

In contrast with the deductive approach, inductive reasoning proceeds from the specific to the general. Observations or measurements are made of a number of cases and, if a common property is found in all cases, a general truth or statement is asserted as applicable to all cases.

The first step in using inductive reasoning to formulate accounting theory consists in deciding what to observe. One possibility, suggested by Schrader, is to observe the financial data generated in business transactions.[19] Littleton, on the other hand, suggested that accounting principles can be inductively derived from experience-tested accounting actions.[20] Observation of the data seems appropriate to the inductive method, while observation of accounting actions seems more in keeping with the practical approach already discussed since the actions of the accountant may change if he knows he is being observed.[21]

Note that the inductive approach necessarily involves a deductive determination of what to observe. It also, out of necessity, embraces certain assumptions — namely, the existence of a separate accounting entity and that all data are to be measured in terms of a standard unit.[22]

The Inductive Approach Illustrated

Assume that the function of accounting is to report upon economic activity. Such activity, to a large extent, is readily observable only in the transactions (loosely defined as exchanges) in which an entity engages. The market price at which such exchanges occur can be readily observed.

Among transactions are those in which goods and services are

[19]William J. Schrader, "An Inductive Approach to Accounting Theory," *The Accounting Review,* Vol. 37 (October 1962), p. 645.

[20]A. C. Littleton, *The Structure of Accounting Theory* (American Accounting Association, 1953), p. 198.

[21]Moonitz, *op. cit.,* p. 6.

[22]Schrader, *op.cit.,* p. 645.

exchanged with a customer for cash or his promise to pay cash. Thus, if the accounting record is to include exchange data, it will contain a monetary quantification of the goods sold or the services rendered – that is, revenues will be recorded at their exchange values. Revenue cannot be recorded earlier since there has been no exchange. It cannot be recorded later since the exchange will then consist of cash for a promise to pay cash rather than for the product delivered or the service rendered. If the goods have not been delivered, or the service rendered, the exchange is a receipt of cash for a promise to deliver – a liability. Thus, a useful generalization emerges – record revenues after an exchange involving the transfer of goods or the rendering of a service.

Advantages of the Inductive Approach

The inductive approach is characterized by freedom. The observer can choose the data he wishes to observe, and if he is not influenced by existing practices, he might respond quickly with new generalizations when new phenomena appear. Careful, open-minded observation can be the source of an immense amount of knowledge.

The principles obtained under the inductive approach have a practical quality which is looked upon favorably by many. They should be in accord with what exists in the real world and so should be immediately useful.

Disadvantages of the Inductive Approach

The approach suffers from the fact that the observer may have preconceived notions of what should be observed or what relationships exist. Or he may have an unconscious bias. Consequently, inductively derived generalizations should be tested by using deductive reasoning.

Another deficiency lies in the fact that the conclusions are derived from a limited number of observations. It is thus entirely possible that the conclusion drawn is false simply because important data were not observed. A question can also be raised as to whether conclusions derived from observation of the data generated by one entity can be applied to the data of yet another entity. And, if measurements are involved, some doubt may exist as to their accuracy.

Finally, simple empiricism may not provide sufficient information on an activity with which the accountant is concerned. For example, the acquisition and disposition of a building can be readily observed, especially if it is physically destroyed at the end of its useful life. But the gradual expiration of the economic properties of the building cannot be measured accurately or observed. And so the inductive approach cannot stand alone as the basis for the vitally necessary periodic reporting found in accounting.[23]

THE ETHICAL APPROACH

Scott advocated that justice, truth, and fairness are the proper concepts upon which accounting principles rest. Accounting principles are general statements which relate accounting rules and procedures to these basic social concepts.[24]

Scott listed three primary principles:

1. Justice: Accounting procedures are to yield equitable treatment for all interests in financial situations covered by the accounts.
2. Truth: Accounting reports should present a true and accurate statement of information.
3. Fairness: Accounting procedures should be fair, unbiased, and impartial.

He also added that accounting procedures should change to bring about adherence to the above principles as economic conditions change, and that accounting procedures should not be changed arbitrarily to serve a temporary purpose.[25]

More recently, Spacek has commented:

My own view is that the one basic accounting postulate underlying accounting principles may be stated as that of fairness—fairness to all segments of the business community . . . , determined in the light of economic and political environment and the modes of thought and customs of all segments—to the end that the accounting principles based upon this postulate shall produce financial accounting for the lawfully established economic rights and interests that is fair to all segments.[26]

The Ethical Approach Illustrated

Scott's principles have already been presented. Of those advo-

[23] *Ibid.,* p. 649.
[24] D. R. Scott, "The Basis for Accounting Principles," *The Accounting Review,* Vol. 16 (December 1941), p. 342.
[25] *Ibid.,* pp. 342–344.
[26] "Comments of Leonard Spacek," in Moonitz, *op. cit.,* p. 57.

cated, he considered his principle of justice as the cornerstone of accounting theory and practice since accrual accounting, the distinction between assets and expenses, and similar fundamental accounting notions are based upon it.

The postulate of fairness is used to support a principle that "liabilities should be recognized and recorded in the period incurred and should be eliminated in the period in which they cease to exist." [27] A careful examination of the interests of management, stockholders, creditors, customers, labor, and the public indicates that a presentation of liabilities and obligations fair to all results when this principle is applied. And the application of the principle calls for the recording and presentation of the liability incurred under long-term leases.[28]

Advantages of the Ethical Approach

Accountants have long recognized the ethical implications of their work. The standard short-form contains the auditor's expression of opinion that the financial statements present fairly the results of operations and financial position. Grady relied heavily upon the concept of fairness in stating the objectives of accounting.[29] Moonitz, while rejecting the ethical approach, stated that "the results of any purposive human activity must be judged in the light of the value judgment inherent in ethical concepts." [30] And the oft-stated accounting requirement of objectivity in the data accumulated is but an attempt to state a standard of impartiality.

Thus, the major advantage of the ethical approach is the statement of worthy goals.

Disadvantages of the Ethical Approach

The approach suffers seriously from the lack of standards to guide its practical implementation. Truth is elusive, even in accounting. For example, does truthful reporting require the disclosure of the historical cost or the approximate current market value of the inventory? Or is it fair to report only a truthful historical cost amount for an important asset if its market value differs substantially?

[27]Arthur Andersen & Co., *The Postulate of Accounting* (Chicago: Arthur Andersen & Co., 1961), p. 37.
[28]*Ibid.*, pp. 41–42.
[29]Grady, *op. cit.*, pp. 57, 62, 65.
[30]Moonitz, *op. cit.*, p. 4.

Similarly, how does one determine whether the accounting data presented are fair and that accounting reports actually do report fairly? A possible test is to determine whether the reports are factual. But the determination of facts is much like ascertaining truth. Two additional tests of fairness have been suggested: (1) that the information presented must be in accordance with generally accepted accounting principles, and (2) that there be full disclosure of comparable data compiled on a consistent basis.[31] But of what value is a model of theory which is to be used to evaluate current practices and principles through application of standards of truth and fairness, when truth and fairness are appraised by conformity to current practice? This circular reasoning destroys the validity of the model.

Consequently, the ethical approach to accounting theory fails because the concepts relied upon are simply too personal, too subjective, and too nebulous.

OTHER APPROACHES AND VIEWS

Yet other views on or approaches to the development of accounting theory exist. These have been stated with varying degrees of completeness and include the following:

1. The axiomatic approach is essentially deductive.[32] It is based on a few axioms and undefined terms and employs mathematical models, expressions, symbols, and proofs. It is yet to be demonstrated that the approach can cope with the problem of valuation in accounting.[33]

2. The communication theory approach defines the accountant's role as observing economic events and reporting them in accounting statements to users, who in turn act and create new economic events.[34] Communication theory is examined for its applicability to accounting, with emphasis on the need to know the user's ability to comprehend information supplied.

[31]Committee on Auditing Procedure, *Auditing Standards and Procedures,* Statements on Auditing Procedures No. 33 (New York: American Institute of Certified Public Accountants, 1963), pp. 69–74. See also Tom K. Cowan, "Are Truth and Fairness Generally Acceptable?" *The Accounting Review,* Vol. 40 (October 1965), pp. 788–794.

[32]The most complete expression of this approach is found in Richard Mattessich, *Accounting and Analytical Method* (Homewood, Ill.: Richard D. Irwin, Inc., 1964).

[33]Moonitz, *op. cit.,* p. 3.

[34]Norton Bedford and Vahe Baladouni, "A Communication Theory Approach to Accountancy," *The Accounting Review,* Vol. 37 (October 1962), pp. 650–659.

3. The closely related sociological and behavioral approaches recognize that persons are motivated by psychological and sociological as well as economic factors.[35] Emphasis is placed upon how individuals, groups, and society are influenced by decisions based on accounting data. Subjective judgment is used to assay the effects of such decisions, but it is still unknown precisely what data are needed to make possible decisions that will benefit the interests of everyone in society.

4. According to one viewpoint, there is no theory of accounting, per se.[36] All that the accountant has, or so it is contended, is his double-entry technique and a few rules for its implementation. His theory consists of ideas taken from other disciplines such as law, economics, statistics, the behavioral sciences, and even biology. Although there is some merit in this contention, it does not explain why only certain ideas are accepted and how ideas taken from different disciplines have a logical relationship in an accounting environment.

5. The theory-is-truth approach states that certain fundamental truths relevant to accounting form the theory of accounting.[37] Diligent searching and logical reasoning will reveal the theorems of accounting — those principles capable of proof. The approach seems to combine tenets of the ethical and axiomatic approaches, with the advantages and disadvantages of both.

6. One contention is that there is no need for a theory of accounting. Holders of this view are quite cynical of attempts to state specific principles or theories, although they acknowledge the existence of some common practices and beliefs which tend to make accounting practices somewhat similar.[38] In a given situation, a proper solution is obtained only through the judgment of one thoroughly experienced in his art. Since it implies intuitive rather than reasoned action on the part of the accountant, this view must be rejected. Only when perception is supported by logical reasoning are reliable measurements of economic activity likely to follow.

---

[35]The sociological approach is found in Dwight R. Ladd, *Contemporary Corporate Accounting and the Public* (Homewood, Ill.: Richard D. Irwin, Inc., 1963); the behavioral approach is found in Thomas R. Prince, *Extension of the Boundaries of Accounting Theory* (Cincinnati: South-Western Publishing Company, 1963).

[36]This view is one which I have encountered rather frequently in graduate theory seminars; it has been espoused primarily by those whose undergraduate education was other than in business or accounting.

[37]Werntz, *op. cit., p. 108.*

[38]*Ibid.*

ACCOUNTING THEORY IN THE FUTURE

Accounting theory consists basically of propositions advanced to guide and explain practice. Currently, opinions differ on which propositions are the proper guides to and explanations of practice; there is disagreement about the approach to theory formulation and no way to demonstrate conclusively that a given proposition should be accepted or rejected. Of course, the present rejection of a proposition in practice does not establish that it is "bad" theory; with time, the theory may be proven sound.

In the deductive model, propositions are accepted or rejected depending upon whether their application helps attain desired objectives. Deductive models are normative models. And the increased reliance upon research to support AICPA pronouncements suggests that accounting theory in the future will be even more normative.[39] In fact, Roy and MacNeill argue that every profession progresses through stages in which knowledge is gained and transmitted through experience, induction, and deduction.[40] But, as the following discussion indicates, not all concur in this view.

THE USES OF THEORY

Accounting theory is often used as a guide to research, an aid in teaching, and a means of acquiring additional knowledge.

Nondirective Uses

According to definition, accounting theory explains and guides practice. Many accountants, however, believe "that theory does not direct; . . . [that it consists] of explanation, definitions, reasons, justifications, persuasions. And only sometimes of suppositions and hypotheses." [41]

Holders of this view tend to emphasize the use of theory in the following:

1. Explaining why a particular practice exists — the amortization of bond premium, for example.

[39] See also *A Statement of Basic Accounting Theory*, pp. 63–71.

[40] Robert H. Roy and James H. MacNeill, *Horizons for a Profession* (New York: American Institute of Certified Public Accountants, 1967), pp. 3–5.

[41] A. C. Littleton, *Essays on Accountancy* (Urbana, Ill.: University of Illinois Press, 1961), p. 376.

2. Persuading that one practice is superior to another—that is, why the accrual basis is preferable to the cash basis.

3. Justifying a particular approach in a given instance—why a merger should be accounted for as a pooling of interests.

4. Explaining why apparently inconsistent and contradictory practices are followed—why, for example, revenue recognition is delayed until cash is received in an accrual basis accounting system.

5. Providing definitions—framing a definition of liabilities in order to exclude the obligation in one contract (a lease) while including the obligation in another (a mortgage note).

Directive Uses

According to others, theory fulfills its most important function when problems are recognized and solutions proposed "by careful attention to what 'ought' to be the case, not what 'is' the case." [42] Paton, for over half a century, wrote that theory should help guide and evaluate practice, as well as examine assumptions on which practices are based; theory, he said, should provide "a little leaven for the loaf of practice." [43] Others are even more forceful. Chambers argues that it is possible to erect a theory of accounting without reference to practice and that "only if theory deals with the ideal can it serve as a guide to developments and improvements in the practice of the related technology." [44]

Theory is used in the following manner in accounting. Every set of auditor's working papers contains possible adjustments— some of very nominal amount—to the client's records. The auditor, for example, may believe that an expenditure which the client charged to expense should be capitalized. He could not reach this conclusion without having some theories regarding the nature of assets and expenses. The fact that he does not pursue the matter further with the client, for practical reasons, does not invalidate the conclusion of theoretical incorrectness. And, by means of auto-

[42]Moonitz, *op. cit.*, p. 6.

[43]W. A. Paton, "Recent and Prospective Developments in Accounting Theory," *Dickinson Lectures* (Cambridge, Mass.: Harvard University Press, 1943), p. 88. See also Herbert F. Taggart, "Remarks on Republication of Paton's Accounting Theory," in W. A. Paton, *Accounting Theory* (Chicago: Accounting Studies Press, Ltd., 1962), p. 7.

[44]R. J. Chambers, "Blueprint for a Theory of Accounting," reprinted in *An Income Approach to Accounting Theory,* Sidney Davidson, David Green, Jr., Charles T. Horngren, and George H. Sorter, eds. (Englewood Cliffs, N. J.: Prentice-Hall, Inc., 1964), p. 58. For his attempt to structure such a theory, see Raymond J. Chambers, *Accounting, Evaluation and Economic Behavior* (Englewood Cliffs, N. J.: Prentice-Hall, Inc., 1966).

mated data processing systems, the impractical of today may be the practical of tomorrow.

But simply because theory is to direct and evaluate practice does not mean that it is unaffected by practice. Theory and practice are not necessarily incompatible; practice tests the validity of theory. For example, during the prosperity of the late 1920s, the current value of many business assets exceeded their historical cost. Many appraisal values were recorded to implement the theory that values were more meaningful than historical costs. But abuses followed. Assets were written up on inadequate evidence and the amount of write-up was reported in a single surplus account or in income.[45] These practices are believed to have contributed to the stock market crash of 1929. During the depression that followed, many assets were written down to market values. These experiences caused accountants in general to reaffirm their belief in historical cost as the proper basis of measurement.

THE ATTRIBUTES OF ACCOUNTING THEORY

What attributes should accounting theory possess? Obviously, it should be useful for some purpose. But such a requirement lacks specificity and leaves the question unanswered. To be useful, accounting theory must possess clarity, impartiality, consistency, completeness, and agreement with empirical evidence. A logical structure of accounting theory can hardly consist of unclear, obscure propositions as lack of comprehension may result and theory is to aid in inducing comprehension. Nor can it contain any proposition that consistently produces biased data, such as the understatement of income (conservatism?). Also, the propositions must be consistent with one another, and, when applied to similar circumstances, they must yield consistent results over time and in accordance with expectations. Again, the propositions should be complete: they should explain and guide all related practices. And the theory related to such a utilitarian technology as accounting can hardly be divorced from reality.

It has also been suggested that sound theory is universal—"that sound accounting principles have world-wide application." [46]

[45]Littleton and Zimmerman, op. cit., pp. 98–99.

[46]Arthur Andersen & Co., Accounting and Reporting Problems of the Accounting Profession, Second Edition (Chicago: Arthur Andersen & Co., 1962), p. 5.

But do they? It has been urged that accounting principles are and should be formulated with reference to the economic, political, and sociological environment, and nations differ in these respects. Yet virtually all societies need some way to measure economic accomplishments. Since this falls within the domain of accounting, at least some accounting principles will have universal application.

SUMMARY

Accounting theory consists of propositions advanced to explain and guide accounting action. The bulk of the propositions currently accepted have been generalized out of accounting practice and are yet to be formulated into a complete body of theory. Most of these propositions have gained acceptance because of the belief that their implementation in practice would produce information useful for some largely unstated objectives.

The essential attributes of a deductive model of theory are a clear statement of objectives and postulates and logically reasoned principles connecting the two. Deductive models focus upon what ought to be rather than what is.

The inductive model is based upon a careful observation of the financial data generated in the flow of economic resources into and out of an enterprise. Patterns of recurring events and relationships are noted from which general conclusions—the principles of the system—are drawn.

In the ethical approach, accounting principles are viewed as applications to accounting of the fundamental social principles of justice, truth, and fairness.

Other attempts to formulate a theory of accounting have relied upon higher mathematics, communication theory, and the sociological and behavioral sciences. And some believe there is no theory of accounting, that there is no need for such a theory, or that theory is truth.

All of the uses of accounting theory are essentially subsumed in the notions that theory is to guide and explain practice. Advocates of the practical approach tend to stress explanation while those supporting deduction stress the normative aspects.

Accounting theory must be useful, and to be useful it must possess clarity, impartiality, consistency, completeness, agreement with empirical evidence, and universality.

QUESTIONS

1. (a) Outline the essential elements in a deductive model of accounting theory. (b) Under this approach, how does one determine the objectives of accounting? (c) What are the major advantages and limitations in this approach?

2. At a recent meeting of accounting practitioners and academicians, a practitioner asserted: "Accounting principles have always been derived from practice, and as far as I can see it will always be this way." (a) Explain why you agree or disagree with this statement. (b) Summarize briefly the major advantages and disadvantages of this approach.

3. In your opinion, why has the accounting profession been unable to state its generally accepted accounting principles?

4. (a) In what respects are the practical and inductive approaches to theory similar? (b) How can they be differentiated?

5. What test is used to evaluate the validity of an alleged principle under the deductive, inductive, practical, and ethical approaches to theory formulation? Explain fully.

6. What is the most important difference between a principle developed in a deductive model and one derived from practice?

7. (a) What has been the general approach of the AICPA to the development of accounting theory? (b) When it granted to the Accounting Principles Board sole authority to speak for it on accounting principles, did the Institute change from its prior approach? Explain fully.

8. Is it in accord with good theory to charge the cost of a wastebasket to expense at the time it is purchased?

9. By what standards are accounting practices to be evaluated under the deductive, inductive, practical, and ethical approaches?

10. What role is played by constraints in the deductive model? Is materiality a constraint? Explain fully.

11. (a) Explain carefully what is meant by the contention that theory is normative. (b) Give an example of what might be called a normative principle of accounting. (c) Are there instances where this principle might not be fully adhered to? Are such practices necessarily "bad" practices? Explain.

12. (a) What are the two major uses of accounting theory? (b) Which do you consider more important? Why?

13. How can accounting principles have universal application when countries differ so widely in form of government, environment, laws, etc.?

14. State what you believe is a principle of accounting and show its development under the practical approach.

15. State what you believe is a principle of accounting and then indicate how you might employ the inductive approach to determine whether, in fact, it is a principle?

16. Construct as much of a deductive model of accounting theory as you consider necessary to show the development of a principle of accounting.

17. Some accountants maintain that accounting and the common law are similar because no list of specific principles or rules exists for either. Have accounting and the common law developed similarly? Explain.

18. Some hold that since theory is logic it cannot contradict itself. Reconcile this position with the use, for the sake of conservatism, of practices that violate the accounting doctrine of consistency.

19. Can a postulate be useful even if it is known to be false? Explain.

2

THE SOURCES OF
ACCOUNTING
THEORY

Selected examples in this chapter illustrate the sources and the development of some of the basic ideas, beliefs, or notions currently guiding accounting practice.

Many factors — economic, institutional, legal, political, sociological, and technological — have influenced the development of of accounting and accounting theory. Because many of these ideas have gained general acceptance slowly, their historical development is briefly presented. Their evolution gives rise to several questions: Were the original objectives in using these ideas the same as the present objectives of accounting? What criteria are used to admit certain concepts to accounting theory and reject others? Agreement on the specific objectives of accounting may well constitute the major hurdle to the development of an acceptable, logical structure of accounting theory.

The following discussion is divided into two major sections — environmental and organizational influences. But such a distinction is purely artificial since many of these factors exerted influences simultaneously and often tended to reinforce each other.

ENVIRONMENTAL INFLUENCES

Double-Entry Bookkeeping

Although the need to account has been cited as the reason for the invention of writing,[1] accounting dates to around the year 1300 and the development of double-entry bookkeeping in the trading centers of Italy.[2] Trade with the East, through the purchase, stock-

[1] Louis Goldberg, *An Inquiry into the Nature of Accounting* (American Accounting Association, 1965), p. 132.

[2] Raymond de Roover, "The Development of Accounting Prior to Luca Pacioli

ing, outfitting, and dispatching of a ship (for accounting purposes – a single venture), provided the impetus for the development of double-entry bookkeeping.

Luca Pacioli's *Suma de Arithmetica, Geometria, Proportioni et Proportionalita* (1494) contained the first published description of double-entry procedure. Even in its earliest application, double-entry bookkeeping embraced certain ideas accepted today, including: (1) the concept of a business entity, (2) the recording of diverse things in terms of money, (3) the need to distinguish between capital and income,[3] and (4) the integration of real and nominal accounts in a single accounting system.[4] And partnership settlement statements from the late 1200s through the 1400s show adjustments for prepaid rent, accrued salaries, taxes, interest, bad debts, and deterioration of equipment.[5]

Continuity of Business Activity

Trade between the new trade centers of western Europe and the western hemisphere slowly became a continuous activity. With continuity came the need to determine profit or loss at the end of each year, a practice proposed by Simon Stevin in 1605. And a legal requirement enacted in France in 1673 (based upon Jacques Savary's recommendation that balance sheets be prepared periodically) required the preparation of a balance sheet by every businessman at least every two years.[6]

The relatively more permanent nature of business activity was also apparent in the 17th century with the formation of the British trading companies under royal charter or act of Parliament. These companies amassed large amounts of permanent capital, which together with continuity of operations made periodic reporting a necessity.[7]

The English Joint Companies Act of 1844 made incorporation

According to the Account-books of Medieval Merchants," in A. C. Littleton and B. S. Yamey (eds.), *Studies in the History of Accounting* (Homewood, Ill.: Richard D. Irwin, Inc., 1956), p. 115.

[3] Eldon S. Hendriksen, *Accounting Theory* (Homewood, Ill.: Richard D. Irwin, Inc., 1965), p. 16.

[4] A. C. Littleton and V. K. Zimmerman, *Accounting Theory: Continuity and Change* (Englewood Cliffs, N.J.: Prentice-Hall, Inc., 1962), p. 47.

[5] Raymond de Roover, "Early Accounting Problems of Foreign Exchange," *The Accounting Review,* Vol. 19 (October 1944), pp. 395ff.

[6] Hendriksen, *op. cit.,* pp. 19–20.

[7] Littleton and Zimmerman, *op. cit.,* pp. 56–57.

by registration possible (with unlimited liability—limited liability came in the act of 1855) and aided the growth of the corporate form. The act required periodic presentation of a "full and fair" balance sheet to stockholders, but not an income statement.[8] The act, and subsequent acts, placed restrictions on dividends and resulted in the adjudication of a number of cases on profits and dividends.[9] And although proper accruals were recognized because of their income rather than their balance sheet effects, little was said about valuation of assets.[10]

Lawrence R. Dicksee's *Auditing* (1892) included the first comprehensive discussion of the going-concern concept of accounting.[11] At that time English law provided that the permanent assets of certain companies, such as those organized to operate canals and railroads, were to be recorded at cost, and dividend statutes generally prohibited increases in plant assets from being paid out in dividends. From these requirements, Dicksee derived the notion that assets were to be valued according to their value to a going concern and divided into two general classes, fixed and floating. Fluctuations in the value of plant assets were of little significance and could properly be ignored since the assets were not to be sold but retained and used in a going business. The valuation of plant assets at cost, as justified by the going-concern concept, quickly received widespread support.[12] But the logical extension of this theory—the valuation of floating assets at their value to a going concern, that is, at their realizable value—was never widely adopted. Conservatism and the absence of realization could not be overcome.[13]

The heavy emphasis in accounting upon objective or verifiable evidence dates to around 1300 in England.[14] This concept also received support from the 1844 act, the 1862 Companies Act, and subsequent acts which required the appointment of auditors and an audit of accounts.[15]

[8] H. C. Edey and Prot Panitpakdi, "British Company Accounting and the Law, 1844–1900," in Littleton and Yamey, *op. cit.*, pp. 356–357.

[9] A. C. Littleton, *Accounting Evolution to 1900* (New York: American Institute Publishing Co., Inc., 1933), pp. 214ff.

[10] *Ibid.*, pp. 151–152.

[11] Reed K. Storey, "Revenue Realization, Going Concern and Measurement of Income," *The Accounting Review,* Vol. 34 (April 1959), p. 233.

[12] *Ibid.*, p. 235.

[13] *Ibid.*, pp. 236–238.

[14] Littleton, *op. cit.*, pp. 260ff.

[15] *Ibid.*, pp. 288–289.

The Influence of the Corporation

The development of the corporation—in addition to supporting the continuity, objectivity, and periodicity concepts—has directly and indirectly influenced the development of accounting theory in a number of ways.

ENTITY THEORY.   In the early 1900s, the accounting for business activity was usually explained through proprietary theory, as found in books by Sprague, Hatfield, and Kester.[16] Under proprietary theory, business activity is viewed through the eyes of the owner of the enterprise. The assets owned and the liabilities owed are those of the proprietor. Income is an increase in proprietorship, and accounting reports are reports to owners.

Such theory was considered appropriate for the smaller enterprise, but for the large corporation entity theory was more suitable. Under entity theory, the business entity is viewed as separate from its owners, with assets and liabilities of its own. Income increases stockholders' equity, which is also a claim against the assets of the entity. Accounting is charged with reporting to all interested parties. Paton is the best known of the early advocates of entity theory.[17]

Current literature contains other theories of the corporation such as the enterprise and residual equity theories.[18]

CONSOLIDATED STATEMENTS AND MERGERS.   The merger wave of 1890–1904 saw the formation of many large corporations, including the U. S. Steel Corporation in 1901, whose annual report for 1902 is considered one of the pioneer consolidated reports in providing reliable information to stockholders.[19] These mergers were responsible for the notions underlying consolidated statements of an economic entity comprised of a number of affiliated corporations. Profits, for example, were not considered realized until

---

[16] Hendriksen, *op. cit.*, pp. 26–27.

[17] William Andrew Paton, *Accounting Theory* (New York: The Ronald Press Company, 1922), Preface, pp. iii, iv.

[18] Waino W. Suojanen, "Accounting Theory and the Large Corporation," *The Accounting Review*, Vol. 29 (July 1954), pp. 391–398, George J. Staubus, *A Theory of Accounting to Investors* (Berkeley and Los Angeles: University of California Press, 1961), Chap. 2.

[19] B. Bernard Greidinger, *Preparation and Certification of Financial Statements* (New York: The Ronald Press Company, 1950), p. 4, as cited by Hendriksen, *op. cit.*, p. 44. See also Percival F. Brundage, "Milestones on the Path of Accounting," *Harvard Business Review*, Vol. 29 (July 1951), p. 72.

goods were sold outside the entity. These mergers also brought about improvements and refinements in accounting procedures, cost accounting, and departmental and product-line accounting.[20]

THE FOUNDATION FOR MODERN FINANCIAL REPORTING. The financial report of U. S. Steel in 1902 was an exception to the general inadequacy of financial reporting at that time. The Westinghouse Electric and Manufacturing Company did not hold an annual meeting or present financial statements to its stockholders during the period 1897 to 1905.[21] As business expanded and the number of stockholders not participating in management increased, the public critics of big business demanded greater disclosure. A leading advocate of greater disclosure was William Z. Ripley.[22]

Hoxsey, on the other hand, criticized business for its accounting practices, especially the use of a number of methods to record depreciation and the use of a variety of techniques to understate income and owners' equity. He also criticized the failure to reveal gross revenues, to report separately material items of other income, to state basic policy underlying consolidated statements (the percentage of ownership of voting stock required before consolidated statements would be prepared), and to state separately the amount of retained earnings.[23] Although largely ignored in the prosperous twenties, these and similar criticisms were mainly responsible for the securities legislation of the depressed thirties.[24]

OTHER INFLUENCES OF THE CORPORATION. The development of the corporation is also at least partially responsible for:

1. Realistic depreciation accounting. This was the result of the legal requirement that dividends be out of income and not out of capital. Capital cannot be maintained or income properly computed without adequate depreciation charges for the expiration of service potential in long-lived assets.
2. The valuation of assets at cost and the resultant shift of attention to

[20] *Ibid.*

[21] David F. Hawkins, "The Development of Modern Financial Reporting Practices among American Manufacturing Corporations," *Business History Review,* Vol. 37 (Autumn 1963), p. 137.

[22] William Z. Ripley, "Stop, Look, Listen!" *Atlantic Monthly,* Vol. 138 (September 1926), p. 380, as cited in Hawkins, *op. cit.,* p. 149.

[23] J. M. B. Hoxsey, "Accounting for Investors," *The Journal of Accountancy,* Vol. 50 (October 1930), pp. 251–284.

[24] Hawkins, *op. cit.,* p. 149.

the income statement and to income as the primary indicator of value.

3. The directing of corporate financial reporting to the stockholder rather than the creditor and the emphasis upon periodic income reporting because of the ready transferability of shares.
4. A number of problems unique to the corporation such as the accounting for treasury stock, stock dividends, stock option plans, and mergers under a pooling-of-interests theory.

Influence of Taxation

The taxation of income by the federal government has influenced the development of accounting practice and theory in many ways in addition to encouraging the maintenance of adequate accounting records.

The 1909 Excise Act levied a tax on net income determined after deducting a reasonable allowance for depreciation.[25] This provision, continued in the Revenue Act of 1913 and in every subsequent act, did much to bring about the recording of depreciation charges and stimulated inquiry into the nature of depreciation and the methods of determining its periodic amount. Similarly, the 1954 act, permitting the use of accelerated methods of computing depreciation, brought accounting acceptance of these methods and greatly widened the theoretical discussion of their merits. And their acceptance for tax purposes helped lead to the development of the theory and practice of allocating income taxes to various time periods.

Section 212(b) of the 1918 act contained provisions, still found in the Internal Revenue Code, requiring taxable income to be determined in accordance with the method of accounting generally employed by the taxpayer unless the method did not clearly reflect income. The act further required taking inventories where needed for a clear reflection of income. Extensive theoretical discussion of the accounting for inventories resulted.

But the greatest effect upon accounting theory of the taxation of income lies in the development of the realization principle. In *Eisner v. Macomber* the Supreme Court said:

Here we have the essential matter; *not* a gain accruing to capital, not a *growth* or *increment* of value *in* the investment; but a gain, a profit, something of exchangeable value *proceeding from* the property, *severed from*

[25] George O. May, *Twenty-five Years of Accounting Responsibility, 1911–1936* (New York: American Institute Publishing Co., Inc., 1936), Part V, p. 277.

the capital however invested or employed, and *coming in* being *derived,* that is *received* or *drawn* by the recipient (the taxpayer) for his *separate* use. . . .[26]

From the transactions approach to the determination of taxable income found in the various acts and from this and other decisions, the idea developed that realization must occur before income emerges. And since realization occurs at time of sale, income is to be recognized then. This method replaced the approach to income determination in which assets are inventoried at the beginning and end of the year.[27] And this change, essentially completed by the early 1930s, reflected the gradual shift in attention from the balance sheet to the income statement.

Another reflection of *Eisner v. Macomber* on accounting theory is the court's position that stock dividends in the same class of shares are not income to the recipient.

A further direct contribution of tax rules is the accounting practice, and its underlying theory, of delaying recognition of revenue and income from installment sales until cash is collected.[28] Also, the fact that a lessee has treated a certain lease as a purchase for tax purposes is cited as justifying—a position many would question—the capitalization for accounting purposes of certain leases.[29] And the existence of provisions in the Internal Revenue Code permitting certain combinations to be "tax free" undoubtedly encouraged the development of the pooling-of-interests theory of accounting for business combinations.[30]

The income tax regulations have had other effects of questionable desirability. LIFO and the various accelerated depreciation methods are accepted today because of tax regulations and are applied indiscriminately in many instances without regard to their theoretical propriety. Assets such as those resulting from research and development expenditures and from partial replacements of

[26] 255 U.S. 189, 193. (Italics in original.)

[27] *Audits of Corporate Accounts* (New York: American Institute of Accountants, 1934), pp. 5–7, 14, 25–26.

[28] George R. Husband, "Receivables," in *Accountants' Handbook,* 3rd ed., W. A. Paton (ed.) (New York: The Ronald Press Company, 1948), p. 417.

[29] Accounting Principles Board, "Reporting of Leases in Financial Statements of Lessee," *Opinion No. 5* (New York: American Institute of Certified Public Accountants, 1964), p. 31.

[30] Arthur R. Wyatt, "A Critical Study of Accounting for Business Combinations," *Accounting Research Study No. 5* (New York: American Institute of Certified Public Accountants, 1963), p. 41.

plant assets are prematurely expensed to gain a tax benefit. And certain accruals, such as for possible sales discounts and returns and for repairs and maintenance, are excluded from the accounts at least in part because such deductions are not allowed.

Influence of Economic Theory

Although the accountant measures economic activity, accounting theory has not borrowed heavily from economic theory. Yet some similarity of ideas does exist. For example, the economic notion that profit emerges upon exchange of goods bears some resemblance to realization.[31] And Adam Smith's classification of capital into circulating and fixed classes is the equivalent of the accounting classifications of current and fixed assets.[32]

The similarity between the economist's concept of wealth and the accounting concept of assets has been noted by many writers.[33] And there is increasing acceptance among accountants that the present value of an asset is the discounted value of its future services or other benefits — an economic concept.[34]

The direct costing concept, which has received so much recent attention, is an attempt to implement the familiar marginal cost theory of the economist. And, currently, accountants are giving considerable attention to economic concepts of income and capital maintenance; these concepts will be discussed more fully later, and it will be sufficient to note for now that accountants and economists no longer agree that income emerges only when it is realized.[35] Economists now tend to criticize accountants for delaying too long in recognizing changes in assets.[36]

[31] Adam Smith, *The Wealth of Nations* (New York: The Modern Library, Inc., 1937), pp. 262–263.

[32] *Ibid.*, pp. 262–267.

[33] Paton, *op. cit.*, p. 33; James L. Dohr, "Income Divorced from Reality," *The Journal of Accountancy*, Vol. 66 (December 1938), pp. 362–363.

[34] Committee on Accounting Concepts and Standards, *Accounting and Reporting Standards for Corporate Financial Statements and Preceding Statements and Supplements* (American Accounting Association, 1957), p. 4.

[35] As quoted in Hendriksen, *op. cit.*, p. 46. See also Stephen Gilman, *Accounting Concepts of Profit* (New York: The Ronald Press Company, 1939), p. 602, which disagrees that realization is an economic concept.

[36] Sidney S. Alexander, "Income Measurement in a Dynamic Society," *Five Monographs on Business Income*, as cited in Maurice Moonitz, "The Basic Postulates of Accounting," *Accounting Research Study No. 1* (New York: American Institute of Certified Public Accountants, 1961), pp. 42–43.

Influence of the Regulation of Public Utilities and Railroads

As railroads developed in England and the United States in the middle 1800s, they made huge investments in relatively permanent assets, causing considerable attention to be paid to distinguishing between capital and revenue expenditures. Diverse methods were used to provide for the maintenance of capital[37] until in the late 1800s it became common to charge renewals and replacements to expense without recording periodic depreciation.[38] But the Interstate Commerce Commission's 1907 classification of accounts called for recording periodic depreciation charges, determined as a percentage of original cost, on certain types of equipment. These orders, although modified and not fully applied until 1943, stimulated discussion on two important questions: Should property consumption and use be measured currently through depreciation charges or only when the property is retired? On what basis — cost or replacement cost — should such charges be computed?[39]

Also as a result of the 1907 classification, the railroads became leaders in allocating bond discount to the periods of life in the bonds. Such a discount was usually treated as a capital charge and added to the cost of the property acquired with the proceeds of the bond issue.[40] And the Wisconsin Public Service Commission, considered a leader in regulation, required that any remaining debt discount on a refunded issue, together with any call premium paid, be allocated to the periods of life in the new refunding issue.[41] Such a procedure, considered unacceptable by the AICPA for many years, recently received the approval of the Accounting Principles Board in its *Opinion No. 6* (paragraph 19) issued in October 1965.

The regulations of the Federal Power Commission have also left their mark on accounting theory. The notion that the historical cost of the assets on a given entity's books can be carried forward as a valid basis of accountability for another entity (the pooling-of-interests theory) seems definitely to have its origin in public utility

[37] Harold Pollins, "Aspects of Railway Accounting before 1868," in A. C. Littleton and B. S. Yamey (eds.), *op. cit.*, p. 343; A. C. Littleton, *op. cit.*, pp. 227ff.

[38] *Ibid.*, p. 236.

[39] Brundage, *op. cit.*, p. 73.

[40] Robert E. Healy, "Treatment of Debt Discount and Premium upon Refunding," *The Journal of Accountancy*, Vol. 70 (March 1942), p. 201.

[41] Herbert C. Freeman, "The Treatment of Unamortized Discount and Premium on Retirement in Refunding Operations," *The Journal of Accountancy*, Vol. 60 (October 1935), p. 255.

accounting. The term "pooling of interests" was first used by the public utility accounting committee of the Institute in discussing certain then-current decisions in utility rate cases.[42] This theory bears a remarkable resemblance to the FPC's regulation that assets transferred between utilities be recorded in the acquirer's rate base at the cost to the party *first* devoting them to public service. This requirement was developed by the Wisconsin commission in 1931.[43]

The notion that interest is a distribution rather than a determinant of net income owes much of its support, if not its origin, to public utility accounting.[44] The operating income of a utility is computed by deducting from revenues all expenses incurred in serving customers. It represents the income available to all capital providers, including bondholders. Interest, capital losses, and donations are then deducted to arrive at net income to stockholders — a proprietary concept. Similar concepts of entity and stockholder income have long been advocated by Paton and have the support of the American Accounting Association.[45]

Influence of Economic and Social Conditions

DEPRESSION.   In the early 1930s many businesses were incurring operating losses caused in part by heavy depreciation charges on the relatively high recorded bases attached to depreciable assets, had accumulated substantial deficits, and had little hope of operating profitably in the near future. The time and expense involved discouraged the seeking of court-approved reorganizations. Accounting solutions were then sought; the first of these called for the write-down of plant assets to capital surplus (to reduce depreciation charges). But this practice was prohibited by a rule passed by the membership of the Institute in 1934[46] and supported by the Securities and Exchange Commission's *Accounting Series Release*

---

[42] See the October 20, 1945, letter to the Executive Council of the American Institute of Accountants from the Committee on Accounting Procedure reprinted in *The Journal of Accountancy,* Vol. 81 (May 1946), pp. 439–440.

[43] Hendriksen, *op. cit.,* p. 37.

[44] *Ibid.*

[45] Paton, *op. cit.,* pp. 267ff; *Accounting and Reporting Standards for Corporate Financial Statements,* p. 5.

[46] Committees on Accounting Procedure and Terminology, *Accounting Research and Terminology Bulletins,* Final Edition (New York: American Institute of Certified Public Accountants, 1961), p. 11.

No. 1 (1937). The adoption of this rule led to the development of rather standardized quasi-reorganization procedures.

As then developed and still accepted, these procedures generally embrace the writing down of assets. The losses so recognized, together with any accumulated deficits, are charged against capital surplus created by a revision of the capital accounts. Neither retained earnings nor a deficit is to be carried forward. Retained earnings arising after reorganization are footnoted as accumulated since reorganization. Consents must be secured from stockholders and creditors if their interests are to be revised.[47]

INFLATION. The literature of accounting contains numerous references over a long period to the possible effects of changing price levels on accounting measurements. The special attention to this matter after World War I probably resulted in part from Irving Fisher's *The Changing Purchasing Power of Money* (1911).[48] Henry Sweeney's *Stabilized Accounting* (1936) is considered a classic reference on the topic. And the attention directed to the matter beginning in the late 1940s was capped by the AICPA's *Accounting Research Study No. 6* (1963).

Although accounting practice appears relatively unchanged by this literature, the appearance is deceptive. In an income-oriented environment, the primary effects of price level changes attach to cost of goods sold and to depreciation. And LIFO and the accelerated depreciation methods have provided partial, but imperfect, solutions. (There may, of course, be valid reasons, such as declining revenues, for using an accelerated depreciation method.) Because the long-run trend of prices is upward, both methods produce higher charges to expense than alternative methods. But these higher charges would only coincidentally be the same as those resulting from the introduction of adjustments for price level changes.

Growing awareness of the effects of price level changes also caused restatements of the monetary postulate. At one time it was considered that the dollar is a stable unit of measure,[49] then that

[47] Committees on Accounting Procedure and Terminology, *Accounting Research Bulletin No. 43,* Chapter 7(a). See also United States Securities and Exchange Commission, *Accounting Series Releases 15* (1940), *16* (1940), and *25* (1941).

[48] See, for example, Livingston Middleditch, "Should Accounts Reflect the Changing Value of the Dollar?" *The Journal of Accountancy,* Vol. 25 (February 1918), pp. 114–120; W. A. Paton, "Depreciation, Appreciation, and Productive Capacity," *The Journal of Accountancy,* Vol. 30 (July 1920), pp. 1–11.

[49] Paton, *op. cit.,* p. 488.

fluctuations in the value of the dollar could be ignored,[50] and currently that changes in the value of the dollar require adjustment if effects are material.[51]

THE PENSION MOVEMENT. The demand for pension and other retirement benefits is due to a number of factors, including the marked increase in the number and proportion of persons aged 65 and over in our economy; the decline in employment opportunities for the aged due to the transformation from an agricultural to an industrial, urban society; the difficulty in saving, caused by high rates of taxation; and the erosion of savings by inflation.[52] And in 1949 the President's fact-finding board on the impending steel strike emphasized the obligation of employers to provide pensions.[53]

The costs involved ensure that attention will be devoted to the accounting for pensions. For example, by December 31, 1949, the estimated past-service liability for pensions of the U. S. Steel Corporation was $677 million while the market value of its outstanding common stock was only $692 million.[54] And for the economy as a whole, private pension plans covering 26 million workers had $90 billion of reserves at the end of 1966.[55]

The search for proper accounting for pensions has produced a host of unresolved questions dealing with such fundamentals as the nature of assets, liabilities, and expense. Does a recordable liability exist when a pension agreement is signed which calls for pensions based in part upon prior service? If a liability is recognized, what account is to be charged? Is the interest paid on unfunded past service costs an operating or nonoperating expense? Many

[50]Study Group on Business Income, *Changing Concepts of Business Income* (New York: The Macmillan Company, 1952), p. 20.

[51]Paul Grady, "An Inventory of Generally Accepted Accounting Principles for Business Enterprises," *Accounting Research Study No. 7* (New York: American Institute of Certified Public Accountants, 1965), p. 370. The author has seen unqualified opinions rendered by certified public accountants on the financial statements of Brazilian companies with such statements adjusted for price level changes. Inflation in Brazil had averaged 62 per cent per year in the five years ending with 1966; Everett J. Mann, "Inflation and Accounting in Brazil," *The Journal of Accountancy,* Vol. 124 (November 1967), p. 49.

[52]Ernest L. Hicks, "Accounting for the Cost of Pension Plans," *Accounting Research Study No. 8* (New York: American Institute of Certified Public Accountants, 1965), pp. 93–94.

[53]*Ibid.,* p. 99.

[54]Brundage, *op. cit.,* p. 79.

[55]*U. S. News and World Report,* "Now Private Pensions Are in the Line of Fire," March 6, 1967, p. 67.

answers are forthcoming, despite Institute attention to the problem (*Accounting Research Bulletins 38, 43,* and *47; Accounting Research Study No. 8;* and *Accounting Principles Board Opinion No. 8*).

Other environmental factors have influenced the development of accounting, including:

1. The development of cost accounting and its areas of concern — inventory valuation, overhead assignment, standard costs — was induced by the industrialization of the United States, and to a lesser extent of England, beginning in the late 1800s.[56]
2. How the development of pooling-of-interests theory was furthered by the desire of professional management to make a good impression and of accountants to avoid reporting substantial amounts of intangible assets.[57]
3. The current attention paid to the financial reporting of widely diversified, industrial empires (conglomerates), as will be discussed briefly later.

ORGANIZATIONAL INFLUENCES

American Institute of Certified Public Accountants

This institute (and its predecessor, the American Institute of Accountants), an organization composed largely of accounting practitioners, has long sought to influence the development of accounting practice and theory. Some of these activities are discussed below.

"UNIFORM ACCOUNTING" AND ITS REVISIONS.   At the request of the Federal Trade Commission, an Institute committee suggested procedures for standardizing the preparation of financial statements for credit purposes. The committee's report was published first as "Uniform Accounting" in the *Federal Reserve Bulletin* (April 1917),[58] again virtually unchanged by the Federal Reserve Board in 1918, and once again in 1929 in a revised edition.[59] These

---

[56]Hendriksen, *op. cit.,* pp. 27–32; Littleton and Zimmerman, *op. cit.,* p. 160.

[57]Leonard Spacek, "The Treatment of Goodwill on the Corporate Balance Sheet," *The Journal of Accountancy,* Vol. 117 (February 1964), p. 38.

[58]Vol. 3, pp. 270–284. Also in *The Journal of Accountancy,* Vol. 23 (June 1917), pp. 401–433.

[59]*Verification of Financial Statements* (Revised), (Washington: U. S. Government Printing Office, 1929). Also in *The Journal of Accountancy,* Vol. 47 (May 1929), pp. 321–354.

reports emphasized (1) providing information to creditors, especially in the balance sheet treatment of current assets and current liabilities (suggested forms for income statements were also presented); (2) valuing inventories at cost or market, whichever is lower; (3) disclosing the fact that plant assets are reported at appraised values; (4) considering depreciation a deduction from income along with taxes and interest; (5) determining profit or loss for the period by adding special credits to, and deducting special debits from, net income for the period; (6) treating prior-period adjustments as additions to or reductions of retained earnings; and (7) using a combined income and retained earnings statement.

"Uniform Accounting" was not warmly welcomed. Bankers feared the loss of clients if too much pressure was exerted for audited statements, and businessmen feared being placed at a competitive disadvantage by providing the disclosure recommended.[60]

The 1929 statement, revised and published by the Institute in 1936,[61] noted the additional use of audited statements as progress reports on management to stockholders, emphasized cost as the basis of asset valuation and consistency in the application of accounting procedures, and stressed the importance of earning power as the source of value and the notion that the balance sheet contains residuals after determining periodic income statement amounts.

COOPERATION WITH THE NEW YORK STOCK EXCHANGE. In 1930 the Institute, primarily at the long-standing urging of J. M. B. Hoxsey and George O. May, appointed a committee with May as chairman, to cooperate with the NYSE on matters of common interest to accountants, investors, and the exchanges.[62] Prior efforts of the NYSE had been directed at securing greater disclosure through a more frequent issuance of financial statements.[63] In a letter,[64] the Institute's committee recommended that the exchange seek to (1) inform the public that a balance sheet does not show present values for assets and liabilities; (2) emphasize the historical nature of the balance sheet and encourage disclosure

[60]Hawkins, op. cit., p. 156.

[61]Examination of Financial Statements by Independent Public Accountants (New York: American Institute of Accountants, 1936).

[62]Paul Grady (ed.), Memoirs and Accounting Thought of George O. May (New York: The Ronald Press Company, 1962), pp. 57ff.

[63]Hawkins, op. cit., p. 150.

[64]Audits of Corporate Accounts, op. cit., pp. 4–18.

of the bases of asset valuation; (3) emphasize that the value of a business depends upon its earning capacity and that the income account is therefore of primary importance; and (4) bring about the universal adoption of a few broad principles of accounting and within such principles make no attempt to otherwise restrict the choice of accounting methods.[65]

The committee further recommended five "broad" principles: (1) only profits realized through sale are to be included in income; (2) capital surplus is not to be charged with items ordinarily charged to expense in current or future periods; (3) the retained earnings shown on a consolidated statement are not to include the retained earnings of a subsidiary prior to its acquisition by the parent company; (4) dividends on treasury stock are not to be credited to income; and (5) amounts due from officers, employees, and affiliated companies are to be stated separately.[66] In 1934 the Institute adopted the five rules, and added a sixth—property received in exchange for stock issued was not to be valued at the par value of the shares issued if some of the shares were donated back to the issuing company. These six rules were published in September 1939 as *Accounting Research Bulletin No. 1.*[67] The *Bulletin* also contained a recommendation that transactions in treasury shares not be allowed to increase the retained earnings account, directly or through the income account.

THE ACCOUNTING RESEARCH BULLETINS.   Attempting to state principles that would become generally accepted, the Institute's Committee on Accounting Procedure issued 51 bulletins over a 20-year period ending with *Bulletin No. 51* in August 1959. In 1953, 31 of the first 42 bulletins were codified into *Accounting Research Bulletin No. 43*. Eight of the remaining bulletins were published in 1953 as *Accounting Terminology Bulletin No. 1;* and the remaining three dealt with wartime problems and are no longer applicable. The bulletins seldom moved ahead of existing practice in their recommendations. *Bulletin No. 51,* advocating the equity method of accounting for unconsolidated subsidiaries, was a rare exception.

While the bulletins usually provided alternative answers to specific problems, a general pattern did emerge. (1) Revenue is to be

---

[65]*Ibid.*, pp. 12–13.
[66]*Accounting Research and Terminology Bulletins*, pp. 11–12.
[67]*Ibid.*, pp. 13–14.

recorded upon its realization, which is usually at the time of sale. (2) Assets are to be valued at not more than cost. (3) Expenses are to be recorded in the periods benefited (the matching notion), and income is to be reported under the current operating concept. (4) Full disclosure and proper classification are essential ingredients in adequate financial reporting.

But the problem-by-problem approach of the bulletins failed to provide the desired structured body of generally accepted accounting principles.[68] Often, a variety of practices was accepted. In other circumstances, the bulletins lacked specificity — for example, Chapter 4 of *Bulletin 43* requires only that the method of determining the cost of inventory clearly reflect periodic income.

THE NEW APPROACH.   In 1959 the Institute created the Accounting Principles Board and an accounting research division as part of a program "to advance the written expression of accounting principles" and "to determine appropriate practices and to narrow the areas of difference and inconsistency in practice." [69] Immediate attention was to be given to determining basic postulates and broad principles. Rules were to be formulated to guide the application of the principles, and the entire program was to be solidly based upon research.

The Board was designated as the Institute's sole authority for public pronouncements on accounting principles. Any topic on which the Board is to act is to be thoroughly studied by investigators from the research staff under the Director of Accounting Research. The results of the studies are to be circulated widely prior to Board action for comment and discussion. The Board may then, at its discretion, issue an official statement — and Opinion.

Through mid-1968, nine research studies had been published. Their numbers and the topics discussed are as follows: *No. 1,* postulates; *No. 2,* cash flow and funds flow; *No. 3,* principles; *No. 4,* leases; *No. 5,* business combinations; *No. 6,* price level effects; *No. 7,* principles; *No. 8,* pensions; and *No. 9,* tax allocation. Of the twelve numbered opinions issued through mid-1968, only five deal with topics previously covered in research studies: *Opinion No. 3,* funds; *Nos. 5* and *7,* leases; *No. 8,* pensions; and *No. 11,*

[68]Reed K. Storey, *The Search for Accounting Principles* (New York: American Institute of Certified Public Accountants, 1964), p. 64.

[69]*Organization and Operation of the Accounting Research Program and Related Activities* (New York: American Institute of Certified Public Accountants, 1959), p. 9.

tax allocation. Of the remaining opinions, *No. 1* deals with depreciation guidelines, *Nos. 2* and *4* with the investment credit, *No. 6* with the status of the *Accounting Research Bulletins,* and *No. 9* with reporting on the results of operations; *Nos. 10* and *12* are omnibus opinions dealing with a variety of minor points relating to pooling of interests, tax allocation, discount on convertible securities, disclosure of depreciable assets and depreciation, deferred compensation contracts, capital changes, and debt issued with stock warrants.

In contrast to the piece-meal approach in the *Accounting Research Bulletins,* the new program, as originally planned, has produced research studies (except *No. 7*) based largely upon deductive reasoning. The Board's opinions have been more solidly founded upon research; they are not simply a consensus of the unsupported opinions of its members. And the opinions contain considerable discussion of alternatives and the reasoning underlying the position taken. A theory structure consisting of broad principles founded on basic postulates has not developed, owing at least in part to disagreement with the postulates of *Study No. 1,* the principles in *Study No. 3,* and in the implications drawn. And the Board has been forced to revert to the problem-by-problem approach to supply guidance on current practical problems. In spite of this reversion and some doubts about whether the Board has the authority to dictate accounting practices,[70] the new program is praiseworthy at least for its research foundation.[71]

The American Accounting Association

One of the stated objectives of the American Accounting Association, an organization primarily of accounting instructors, is to influence the development of accounting theory. Its more important attempts to do so can be found in a number of publications, including a series of statements on accounting principles, standards, and theory.[72]

---

[70] These issues were resolved, at least for the Institute and its members, by the Institute Council's adoption of a recommendation calling for disclosure of departures from Board opinions for fiscal periods beginning after December 31, 1965. See *The Journal of Accountancy,* Vol. 117 (November 1964), pp. 11–12.

[71] Storey, *op. cit.,* p. 58.

[72] For a complete and interesting history of the Association, see Stephen A. Zeff, *The American Accounting Association — Its First Fifty Years* (Evanston, Ill.: American Accounting Association, 1966).

THE 1936 STATEMENT AND REVISIONS. "A Tentative Statement of Accounting Principles Underlying Corporate Financial Statements" was published by the Executive Committee of the Association in 1936. It was the first effort by an American accounting organization to set forth a consistent, coordinated statement of accounting principles. The statement was revised and published in 1941 and again revised and published in 1948. Eight supplemental statements were published from 1950 to 1954, dealing with reserves and retained income, price level changes, current assets and current liabilities, accounting principles and taxable income, accounting corrections, inventory prices and price level changes, consolidated statements, and disclosure. The last revision in this series is entitled "Accounting and Reporting Standards Underlying Corporate Financial Statements — 1957 Revision." [73] Two numbered supplementary statements — *No. 1* on long-lived assets and *No. 2* on inventories — were published in 1964.[74] Three unnumbered committee reports on concepts stated in the 1957 revision (entity, realization, and matching) were published in 1965.[75]

Some of the important recommendations and developments in this series of statements are the following:

1. The statements show a distinct trend away from prescribing detailed rules to combat improper practices (e.g., treasury stock is to be reported as a deduction in stockholders' equity and not as an asset) toward presenting broad principles (realization) and basic underlying concepts (entity).

2. The 1936 statement (and to a lesser degree, the 1941 and 1948 statements) heavily emphasized cost as the proper basis of valuation of assets, asserting that accounting is an allocation process, not a valuation process. The statement sought to discourage the rather common practice of revising asset values as economic conditions changed. Not until the 1957 revision were the definition and measurement of assets divorced from cost. The 1964 supplements both go further and recommend the use of replacement or current cost in measuring assets for isolating holding gains and losses.[76]

[73] All of the above listed statements were published in *Accounting and Reporting Standards for Corporate Financial Statements and Preceding Statements and Supplements.*

[74] See *The Accounting Review,* Vol. 39 (July 1964), pp. 693–699 and 700–714.

[75] See *The Accounting Review,* Vol. 40 (April 1965), pp. 312–322, 358–367, and 368–372.

[76] For a full discussion of the concept of holding gains and losses, see Edgar O. Edwards and Philip W. Bell, *The Theory and Measurement of Business Income* (Berkeley and Los Angeles: University of California Press, 1961), esp. Chapters 2 and 3.

3. The 1936 statement stressed the need to recognize depreciation; the 1941 statement recommended, in effect, the recording of straight-line depreciation as a minimum requirement; the 1948 statement called for a reasonable approach to recording depreciation as an expense and for the balance sheet to show only amounts properly carried forward; the 1957 revision related depreciation to the decline in the service potential of an asset; and the 1964 supplement defined depreciation as an expiration of service potential.

4. The 1936, 1941, and 1948 statements contain increasingly strong recommendations for the all-inclusive concept of income. This concept was undoubtedly supported in the hope that the additional disclosure it affords would eliminate some of the confusion, inconsistency, and bias surrounding the determination and treatment of extraordinary gains and losses. And the desire to eliminate possible sources of income manipulation was responsible for the position taken in the 1948 statement that an assignment to expense could not be corrected in later years when found to be erroneous if the original assignment was made in good faith.[77] The 1957 revision does not support the all-inclusive concept as strongly since it excludes from periodic income those items recognized in the current period which relate to prior periods.[78]

THE 1966 STATEMENT. A new approach to theory formulation was taken by the Committee to Prepare a Statement of Basic Accounting Theory.[79] Rather than dealing with familiar concepts — entity, realization, continuity — the committee determined the attributes that information must possess to be useful in accounting. These attributes were relevance, verifiability, freedom from bias, and quantifiability. Five guidelines to communication were also presented.[80]

Uniquely, the report's theory included management accounting and accounting in the not-for-profit sector. Typically, accounting theory and financial accounting theory are equated. The report also placed heavy emphasis upon providing information useful in pre-

[77] This provision drew vigorous criticism; see for example W. A. Paton "The 1948 Revision of the American Accounting Association's Statement of Principles: Comments on Item 5, under 'Expense,' " *The Accounting Review,* Vol. 24 (January 1949), pp. 49–53. As a result, it was revised somewhat in *Supplementary Statement No. 5.*

[78] For a more complete analysis of these statements, see Hendriksen, *op. cit.,* pp. 67–72; also Harvey T. Deinzer, *The American Accounting Association Sponsored Statement of Standards for Corporate Financial Reports: A Perspective* (Gainesville, Fla.: Accounting Department, College of Business Administration, University of Florida, 1964).

[79] *A Statement of Basic Accounting Theory* (Evanston, Ill.: American Accounting Association, 1966).

[80] *Ibid.,* pp. 8–18.

diction. The committee's major recommendations on reporting to external users were (1) the presentation of multicolumn financial statements for reporting historical and current cost; (2) the classification of expenses in income statements into fixed and variable classes; and (3) the reporting of assets, expenses, and revenues by product or division lines.[81]

OTHER PUBLICATIONS. Since 1937 the Association has published monographs on (1) public utility depreciation, (2) financial statements, (3) corporate accounting standards, (4) consolidated statements, (5) accounting theory, (6) auditing philosophy and evidence, and (7) the nature of accounting. Monograph No. 3, *An Introduction to Corporate Accounting Standards,* has become one of the most widely quoted classics of American accounting literature.[82] The monograph was written by two members of the committee that prepared the 1936 statement.[83]

The Association's concern over the possible effects upon accounting measurements of price level changes can be noted in its statements on principles, standards, or theory and in three publications during 1955–56.[84]

Securities Legislation and the Securities and Exchange Commission

The passage of the Securities Act of 1933 and the Securities Exchange Act of 1934 (which created the Securities and Exchange Commission to administer these and subsequent acts) has been cited as one of the most important steps in the development of accounting principles.[85] These acts gave the SEC authority to

[81] *Ibid.,* pp. 30–32.

[82] Zeff, *op. cit.,* p. 57.

[83] W. A. Paton and A. C. Littleton, *An Introduction to Corporate Accounting Standards* (American Accounting Association, 1940).

[84] Ralph Coughenour Jones, *Price Level Changes and Financial Statements—Case Studies of Four Companies* (American Accounting Association, 1955); R. C. Jones, *Effects of Price Level Changes on Business Income, Capital, and Taxes* (American Accounting Association, 1956); Perry Mason, *Price-Level Changes and Financial Statements* (American Accounting Association, 1956).

[85] Carman G. Blough, "Development of Accounting Principles in the United States," *Berkeley Symposium on the Foundations of Financial Accounting* (Berkeley: Schools of Business Administration, University of California, 1967), p. 3. (Mr. Blough was the SEC's principal staff accountant from December 1934 to November 1935 and its Chief Accountant from December 1935 to June 1938.)

prescribe, in whatever detail it desires, the accounting practices and principles to be employed by companies required to file financial statements with it. The SEC's published requirements and opinions on accounting matters can be found in (1) its *Accounting Series Releases,* 110 of which have been issued since April 1, 1937, dealing with a variety of accounting matters; (2) Regulation S-X, first promulgated in 1940 and detailing instructions and forms for filing financial statements with the Commission; and (3) decisions on matters presented formally to the Commission.[86]

Yet the influence of the securities legislation and the SEC has been largely indirect due to the policy adopted in *Accounting Series Release No. 4.*

ACCOUNTING SERIES RELEASE NO. 4.   In the first six months of 1935, the financial statements of over 2,500 companies were filed with the SEC and became available to the public. For the first time, the diversity in accounting practices among businesses was fully revealed.[87] The resulting criticism, defense, analysis, and discussion gave considerable impetus to the search for accounting principles.

After its Chief Accountant dissuaded it from prescribing accounting principles, the Commission adopted the present policy of cooperating with the profession, especially the Institute, in developing accounting principles.[88] The Commission's *Accounting Series Release No. 4* (April 25, 1938) stated that financial statements "prepared in accordance with accounting principles for which there is no substantial authoritative support" will be considered misleading regardless of disclosures. And where the Commission and the registrant disagree on proper principles, "disclosure will be accepted in lieu of correction of the financial statements only if the points involved are such that there is substantial authoritative support for the practices followed," provided such practices do not conflict with the previously expressed position of the Commission.

Immediately, to arrive at "substantial authoritative support," partners of some of the larger CPA firms attempted to reach agreement on a statement of accounting principles. This led to the forma-

---

[86] For an extended discussion of Commission requirements and actions, see Louis H. Rappaport, *SEC Accounting Practice and Procedure* (2nd edition)(New York: The Ronald Press Company, 1963).

[87] Blough, *op. cit.,* p. 4.

[88] *Ibid.,* p. 5.

tion in 1938 of the Institute's Committee on Accounting Procedure.[89] But what constitutes "substantial authoritative support" remains unresolved even today.

EVIDENCE OF COOPERATION.   The Commission and the accounting profession have genuinely cooperated. On one occasion an item was dropped from the agenda of the Committee on Accounting Procedure as a result of objections from the Chief Accountant of the SEC.[90] In another instance, numerous objections were made to the SEC's 1950 proposal to revise Regulation S-X to include (1) the definition of a quasi-reorganization as a downward adjustment vehicle only; (2) the policy in Release No. 4; (3) a requirement to state assets generally at cost; and (4) a requirement to use the all-inclusive income concept.[91] Resolutions passed at the annual meetings of both the Institute and the American Accounting Association objected primarily to the proposed change in SEC policy, although the Institute also objected to the proposed requirement for reporting income under an all-inclusive concept. As a result of these objections all references to accounting principles were dropped from the revision, a general reference was made to all *Accounting Series Releases,* and a compromise form of income statement was developed.

Much of the original impetus to inquire into the adequacy of the financial reporting practices of widely diversified companies (conglomerates) came from the SEC. In this inquiry, the SEC has sought to cooperate not only with the American Institute but with the Financial Executives Institute and other organizations.[92] And the Senate Subcommittee on Antitrust and Monopoly has played a key role in directing and supporting the SEC's questioning of whether conglomerates should be required to report sales and earnings by divisions as well as on a consolidated basis.[93]

---

[89] *Ibid.,* p. 7.

[90] *Ibid.,* p. 9.

[91] Andrew Barr, "The Influence of Government Agencies on Accounting Principles with Particular Reference to the Securities and Exchange Commission," an address at the 37th annual Michigan Accounting Conference of the MACPA at the University of Michigan, Ann Arbor, October, 18, 1963. Reprinted in *The Michigan CPA,* Vol. 15 (March–April 1964), pp. 5–14.

[92] "News Report," *The Journal of Accountancy,* Vol. 122 (November 1966), p. 9.

[93] "Market Brief," *Business Week,* May 28, 1966, p. 152, as cited in Stephen A. Zeff, "Comments on 'Development of Accounting Principles in the United States' by Carman G. Blough," *Berkeley Symposium on the Foundations of Financial Accounting,* p. 22.

COST BASIS OF VALUATION.   The SEC has always required the cost basis of valuation for assets — a practice not universally accepted at its inception. This action was apparently influenced by the arguments of one of the commissioners, who had been chief counsel in the Federal Trade Commission's investigation into the write-up malpractices of public-utility holding companies in the 1920s.[94] Many of the decisions in the early formal hearings before the Commission required the restatement of assets at cost and the removal of substantial amounts of intangible values recorded by valuing properties received at the par value of the shares of stock issued in exchange. The position developed, together with the desire to prevent the reporting of substantial amounts of intangible assets, probably accounts for the Commission's avid support of pooling-of-interests theory.[95]

SEC LEADERSHIP.   The SEC has, on occasion, taken the lead in promoting certain practices. For example, *Accounting Research Bulletin No. 24* (December 1944) sought only to discourage rather than prohibit the practice of writing off goodwill to capital surplus. But *Accounting Series Release No. 50* (January 1945) went further and stated flatly that this practice was not in accord with "sound" (note — sound, not generally accepted) accounted principles. Subsequently, *Accounting Research Bulletin No. 43* (June 1953) barred the charging of purchased goodwill to capital surplus.[96]

The SEC's *Accounting Series Release No. 102* (December 1965) in effect required a current liability classification for that portion of the deferred federal income taxes account relating to installment receivables classified as current assets. Practice at that time permitted classification of the account as a current liability, a long-term liability, between liabilities and stockholders' equity, and below stockholders' equity. Of course, classification as a current liability affected reported working capital.[97]

A similar provision, approved by the Accounting Principles

[94] Blough, *op. cit.*, p. 10; Zeff, *op. cit.*, p. 21.

[95] George Catlett, "Current Efforts to Define Accounting Principles," an address at the Michigan Accounting Educators' Conference, Eastern Michigan University, April 22, 1967.

[96] Andrew Barr, "Accounting Aspects of Business Combinations," *The Accounting Review*, Vol. 34 (April 1959), p. 177. Mr. Barr was then and is now Chief Accountant for the SEC.

[97] See the speech by Manuel F. Cohen, Chairman of the SEC, reprinted in *The Journal of Accountancy*, Vol. 122 (August 1966), p. 59.

Board in a June 1965 meeting, had been included in an exposure draft of *Opinion No. 6*. But the provision was deleted from the formal opinion because it was felt that *Opinion No. 6* (dealing with the status of the *Accounting Research Bulletins*) was not the proper vehicle to introduce new requirements.[98] The failure of the Board to act at this time caused a large CPA firm to petition the SEC for a ruling. And by its issuance of *Release No. 102*, the SEC has indicated its willingness to act if the Board does not.

A CONCLUDING OBSERVATION

This chapter has illustrated how accounting theory has developed from ideas and practices of many disciplines, conceived to meet a variety of objectives. The fact that these objectives have varied and often conflicted probably explains why a logical body of accounting theory for general-purpose financial statements has not been formulated. For example, without specific inquiry into creditor information needs, it may not be appropriate to proceed on the premise that a practice accepted for tax purposes — LIFO — automatically produces information useful to creditors. Nor does it follow that stockholders can rely upon information produced by applying principles and practices accepted, at least in part, because they make management look good.

Consequently, a clear-cut statement of objectives would seem to be of paramount importance in formulating accounting theory. And, if multiple objectives are recognized, criteria must be included to ensure that principles and practices selected are consistent with objectives.

QUESTIONS

1. (a) Which of the various sources of influence discussed in this chapter has had the greatest impact in shaping current accounting practices and theories? (b) Why has this apparently been the major source of influence? (c) Provide several additional examples of how this source influenced the development of accounting theories and practices.

2. (a) Define the relationship between accounting and its environment. (b) Is it true that accounting is largely the product of disasters, not the product of a slow evolutionary process? Explain.

[98]"News Report," *The Journal of Accountancy*, Vol. 121 (January 1966), p. 8 (quoting Clifford Heimbucher, chairman of the Board).

3. Some accountants believe that a single set of financial statements can and should be prepared and that such statements will supply the information needed by all interested parties. Does the history of accounting suggest that this ideal will ever be attained? Explain.

4. What are the advantages and disadvantages in the development of the ideas currently believed by some to constitute accounting theory? Explain fully.

5. Although current accounting theories and practices are largely responses to diverse needs, are there common threads in these needs? Explain.

6. Indicate with several examples how environmental or organizational influences other than those cited in this chapter have influenced the development of accounting theory.

7. (a) Double-entry bookkeeping has been characterized as one of the finest inventions of the human mind. Do you agree? (b) What are some of the ideas embraced in the earliest examples of double-entry bookkeeping still accepted?

8. Indicate with several examples how different factors combined to influence the development of accounting theory.

9. Trace the development of accounting theory by indicating those whose information needs appear to have been given top priority as accounting responded to demands upon it.

10. (a) What are the essential elements of entity theory? (b) When did it begin to develop in the United States? Why? (c) From what major sources has it received support?

11. Currently, accounting literature warns that if the profession does not quickly respond to demands upon it, others will usurp the accounting function or government will dictate the profession's methods by fiat. Does the history of accounting suggest that either of these alternatives is likely? Explain.

12. (a) On the surface, accounting and economic theories appear to be quite similar since both are concerned with economic activity. In what respects are they similar? (b) Why isn't there greater similarity?

13. Cite six important events or milestones in the history of accounting and explain why you chose each event.

14. What has been the major contribution of the AICPA in the development of accounting theory? Explain.

15. (a) Contrast the different approaches to the development of accounting theory made by the AICPA and the American Accounting Association. (b) Why haven't the AAA's efforts received much support in practice?

16. (a) Indicate several areas of accounting theory in which the Securities and Exchange Commission has been active. (b) Explain why it has played an important role in these areas. (c) Why will the full impact of the Commission upon the development of accounting theory probably never be known?

17. Is it proper to say that accounting principles have evolved? Aren't accounting principles primarily man-made rules subject to change whenever desirable? Discuss.

18. (a) Does double-entry bookkeeping necessarily imply any specific basis of asset valuation? (b) What factors were influential in bringing about acceptance of the historical cost basis of valuation?

19. (a) During what period did emphasis shift from the balance sheet to the income statement? (b) What factors apparently caused this shift?

20. Is accounting a neutral element in the history of business or does it actually help shape business activity?

3

THE BASIC
CONCEPTS

Any persistent study of accounting theory or practice will inevitably lead to the conclusion that certain ideas, explicit or implicit, underlie its principles and practices. The fundamental ideas are usually referred to as concepts, postulates, or assumptions — but the last term tends to be used less frequently in modern literature. These will be discovered through a formal deductive model or a simple inventory of accepted notions. Without some such framework for guidance, the study of accounting becomes nothing more than the memorization of a somewhat nebulous, unintegrated mass of rules of practice.

In this chapter the basic concepts from a pragmatic inventory of accounting principles are presented, and discussed, then contrasted with the basic postulates of a deductive model of theory. The support for the contention that these concepts are basic to accounting is presented with other evidence from accounting literature. The significance of each concept for accounting practice is also briefly given.

To economize in the footnoting of references, the following abbreviations are used throughout the chapter:

Abbreviation	*Reference*
Grady	Paul Grady, "An Inventory of Generally Accepted Accounting Principles for Business Enterprises," *Accounting Research Study No. 7* (New York: American Institute of Certified Public Accountants, 1965).
Moonitz	Maurice Moonitz, "The Basic Postulates of Accounting," *Accounting Research Study No. 1* (New York: American Institute of Certified Public Accountants, 1961).
AAA	Committee on Accounting Concepts and Standards, *Accounting and Reporting Standards for Corporate Financial Statements and Preceding Statements and Supplements* (American Accounting Association,

	1957). Primary reference here is to the 1957 Revision.
Hendriksen	Eldon S. Hendriksen, *Accounting Theory* (Homewood, Ill.: Richard D. Irwin, Inc., 1965).
Paton	William Andrew Paton, *Accounting Theory* (New York: The Ronald Press Company, 1922). Reprinted by A. S. P. Accounting Studies Press, Ltd., 1962.
Paton and Littleton	W. A. Paton and A. C. Littleton, *An Introduction to Corporate Accounting Standards,* American Accounting Association Monograph No. 3 (American Accounting Association, 1st printing, 1940).
Sanders, Hatfield, and Moore	Thomas Henry Sanders, Henry Rand Hatfield, and Underhill Moore, *A Statement of Accounting Principles* (New York: American Institute of Accountants, 1938). Reprinted by the American Accounting Association in 1959.
Theory Statement	Committee to Prepare a Statement of Basic Accounting Theory, *A Statement of Basic Accounting Theory* (Evanston, Ill.: American Accounting Association, 1966).

THE NATURE OF BASIC CONCEPTS

Every discipline or field of knowledge is based upon certain fundamental premises variously referred to as assumptions, concepts, or postulates. For example, according to our law, a man is innocent until proven guilty. The physicist assumes that energy can be neither created nor destroyed; the mathematician that every integer has a successor. And present-day microeconomic theory rests heavily upon the notion of diminishing marginal utility.

These basic concepts are often accepted without proof because they are deemed self-obvious. In other instances, they simply are not capable of proof, or man has yet to devise a means of proving them. These concepts are considered useful and necessary because they (1) form the foundation from which further useful propositions are drawn, (2) prevent an endless delving into the origins of a discipline, (3) prevent circularity in reasoning, and (4) aid in distinguishing the subject matter of the discipline — accounting from chemistry, for example.[1] Typically, these concepts are stated in undefined terms called primitives.

[1] For general disagreement with the approach of stating postulates or concepts and for arguments that matters such as the entity concept are open to inquiry rather than to be assumed, see Harvey T. Deinzer, *Development of Accounting Thought* (New York: Holt, Rinehart and Winston, Inc., 1965), esp. Chap. 9.

The basic concepts of accounting presented by Grady provide the framework for the discussion in this chapter. Considerable evidence supports the contention that the ideas in these concepts influence accounting although they are not always referred to as basic. The most important evidence is the widespread support in the literature of accounting. Further support is provided by the absence of disagreement with the concepts presented (with one exception), either by Grady's project advisory committee or in the literature of accounting.

Grady's list (p. 24) of basic concepts includes (1) a society and government structure honoring private-property rights, (2) specific business entities, (3) going concern, (4) monetary expression in accounts, (5) consistency between periods for the same entity, (6) diversity in accounting among independent entities, (7) conservatism, (8) dependability of data through internal control, (9) materiality, and (10) timeliness in financial reporting requires estimates.

A SOCIETY AND GOVERNMENT STRUCTURE HONORING PRIVATE-PROPERTY RIGHTS

Two ideas are contained in this basic concept. First, accounting principles may differ between the United States and other nations because of differences in the extent to which private-property rights are honored. The accounting principles considered appropriate in accounting for and reporting upon the private ownership of property may have little, if any, applicability in a society where all property is state-owned. Secondly, and more importantly, if private-property rights are to be honored, these rights must be recognized, enforced, and protected by legal means. "Practically every entry made in the accounts of a business entity rests on this concept " (Grady, p. 25).

Although not stressed by Grady, the American accountant seems to rely on legally enforceable property rights to support his current practice of recording for a business entity only resources it has legal title to or which it possesses with the expectation of acquiring legal title. Representations of financial condition properly do and should include only such resources as assets, or so it is contended.

This concept permeates accounting practice in the United States. Our generally accepted accounting principles are framed with consideration for reporting by private business entities to external parties on their ownership, use, interests in, and obligations to pay for economic resources. For this reason, our accounting principles may differ from those adhered to in societies where private ownership of property is not permitted. Also, current accounting practices are heavily influenced by the expectation that contracts, agreements, commitments, and obligations will be adhered to or fulfilled. In fact, it can be maintained that accrual basis accounting is soundly rooted in this concept.

Yet all societies desire knowledge of the efforts expended and the accomplishments secured where economic resources are employed. If accounting is to provide such measurements, it would seem that it cannot be completely dissimilar among societies.[2] And not all entities have legal title to the resources they employ, so the measurements of efforts expended may be incomplete if only legally owned resources are included. This concept is not included in the basic postulates presented by others, probably for the same reasons that Moonitz excludes it from his list. He states that the generalization "we live in an orderly society in which the potential consequences of actions can be predicted with some degree of success" is more basic and underlying than "any others that can be formulated" (Moonitz, p. 21). And although "private ownership of most productive resources" (p. 9) is a characteristic of our economic organization, it is not of direct relevance to accounting since accounting is used "where private ownership is not present" (p. 10).

SPECIFIC BUSINESS ENTITIES

A universally accepted postulate or concept of accounting is that of the existence of a separate entity for which accounts are to be maintained and reports rendered.[3] The assumption may be explicitly stated (Paton, p. 472; Paton and Littleton, p. 8; AAA, p. 2) or implied (Sanders, Hatfield, and Moore, pp. 1, 18). This entity is

[2] For a discussion of accounting in a communist state, see Paul Kircher, "Accounting 'Revolution' in Red China," *Financial Executive*, Vol. 35 (February 1967), pp. 39ff.

[3] The entity concept is given official recognition by the Accounting Principles Board in its "Accounting for Income Taxes," *Opinion No. 11* (New York: American Institute of Certified Public Accountants, 1967), p. 160.

assumed to have an existence apart from its owners, employees, creditors, management, or others who may have an interest in it. Moonitz goes a step further by stating two entity postulates:

Postulate A-3. Entities (including identification of the entity). Economic activity is carried on through specific units or entities. Any report on the activity must identify clearly the particular unit or entity involved.

Postulate B-3. Entities. (Related to A-3). The results of the accounting process are expressed in terms of specific units or entities (p. 52).

Note that Moonitz does not restrict his concept of the entity to the business sector of the economy. A research committee of the American Accounting Association takes a similar position, holding that the term "business entity" is unduly restrictive when discussing underlying concepts of accounting because accounting is carried on in nonbusiness entities.[4]

But what is an entity? An entity is an organization, institution, or unit of activity composed of persons and economic resources joined together to pursue certain express or implied objectives. In a business entity, these objectives are the acquisition of various resources and services, their utilization or transformation, and the ultimate delivery of goods or rendering of services to others with expectation of profit.

Grady discusses only the business corporation as an entity, considers financial statements for a corporate department or division to be "special purpose" rather than statements of a reporting entity, and accepts the consolidated group of corporations as the business entity in which one corporation holds a controlling interest in the voting stock of other corporations (p. 26). He also holds that, when two previously separate entities combine in a pooling of interests, the historical cost basis of accounting of the previously separate entities is appropriate for the continuing enlarged entity (p. 27).

Paton and Littleton stress the importance of the entity concept in accounting for the unincorporated as well as the incorporated business and agree that a section of a business entity is a subordinate form of entity (pp. 8–9).

An American Accounting Association committee extended the entity concept to include political, social, aesthetic, professional,

---

[4]Concepts and Standards Research Study Committee, "The Entity Concept," *The Accounting Review,* Vol. 40 (April 1965), p. 360.

as well as economic entities. The economic entity, with which accounting is concerned, was defined as *"an area of economic interest to a particular individual or group."* [5] Thus, an economic entity may exist for a profit center, a product line, a partnership, a single proprietorship, a corporation, or a group of corporations. And the accountant may maintain records and prepare reports for any of these.

In view of this disagreement, why does the accountant assume the existence of an entity? Because he has no alternative. He must have some idea about what he is reporting upon before he can render any meaningful report. The entity concept, viewed in this manner, is probably the most fundamental and absolutely indispensable concept in accounting.[6]

But, typically, the term "entity" is not used to describe a profit center or a product line. Its traditional environment is in financial accounting and is closely tied to the notion of reporting to persons external to the entity. The American Accounting Association committee has noted that the accountant does account for units of activity which, in the financial accounting sense, are subentities of the larger reporting entity. But the entity concept is still used to determine what data to include and what to exclude. The boundaries of the entity depend solely on the point of view taken. And, since there are many different users of accounting information, with differing points of view, there are many different entities.

A discussion of whether the entity assumed to exist is real or fictional serves no useful purpose. The accountant needs the entity concept to present useful information. No further justification is necessary.

GOING CONCERN (CONTINUITY)

Another basic concept or postulate of accounting is that, in the absence of evidence to the contrary, the entity for which an accounting is undertaken has an indefinite life (Moonitz, pp. 38–41; Paton, pp. 478–480; Paton and Littleton, pp. 9–11; Sanders, Hatfield, and Moore, p. 3; AAA, p. 2). Continuity, and not liquidation, is to be expected. (The concept has a corollary: when an entity has a limited life, it should not be viewed as a going concern.) Most entities are

[5] *Ibid.*, p. 358 (emphasis in original).
[6] *Ibid.*

organized for and do have an indefinite life. Management's decisions to acquire long-lived assets and undertake research expected to bear fruit a number of years hence clearly demonstrate expectation of continuity of operations.

The major effects of adopting the continuity assumption are the avoidance of the liquidation basis of valuation for assets and the inclusion of accruals not legally recognized as liabilities. The possibility that reported net income might be changed significantly (with a resulting change in retained earnings) should be obvious.

For example, work-in-process inventories may be virtually worthless from a liquidation point of view. Yet the accountant will usually carry them at cost (the notions of objectivity and realization usually prevent a higher valuation) and not at liquidation value because he assumes a going concern which will complete and market the goods and recover all costs incurred from the revenues secured. Note also that the continuity assumption enables him to avoid what might be a difficult task—the actual determination of liquidation values.

Similarly, depreciable assets are carried at cost in the expectation that the services of these assets will be consumed in the generation of future revenues sufficient to recover their undepreciated cost. The policy of not amortizing certain assets—organization costs—is based upon the argument that such assets will benefit the entire life of the entity, which is, according to the continuity concept, indefinite.

The relationship between the continuity concept and the recognition of liabilities is equally direct. Liabilities are recorded currently in the accrual of certain expenses, such as pensions, even though no legal obligation exists at that time. The justification is that the benefits have been received in the revenue recognized currently, that future payments will have to be made, and that the entity will continue to operate until payment date arrives.

But the truly significant result of accepting the continuity assumption is that the income statement becomes the primary accounting statement and replaces the balance sheet as the basis for estimating the value of an entity. Entity value is the result of earning power, periodically measured as revenues recognized less costs incurred, not the result of assets owned regardless of methods employed to measure them—cost, replacement cost, market value, etc. And this same earning power is viewed as an indicator of managerial efficiency (Paton and Littleton, p. 10).

The continuity concept is challenged only by those who argue that continuity need not be assumed since it is a verifiable fact.[7] Every entity not actually terminated has some uncompleted transactions for which accounting data are being carried forward to future periods. Continuity is thus a state or condition of the entity, and the accounting data reflect this fact. But since asset values are affected by assumptions about the future and since not every entity can be expected to have an indefinite life, the users of financial statements are entitled to know whether they have been prepared under the assumption of indefinite continuity or near-term liquidation (Hendriksen, p. 88). Continuity may be assumed in the absence of information to the contrary.

Financial statements are validly based upon an expectation of continuity because the accountant has no alternative, except where termination is known and planned. He cannot let his personal beliefs about an entity's ability to survive cause him to discard the going-concern point of view. No matter how strongly he believes it to be true, he cannot represent that an entity, even one in serious financial difficulty, is not likely to survive. Such a representation would probably serve only to ensure the demise of the entity by inducing adverse actions against it, such as creditor foreclosures or denials of additional credit. He must assume the entity will adapt itself to its environment and survive unless management intends to terminate it.

MONETARY EXPRESSION IN ACCOUNTS

The basic data of accounting are the money measurements or bargained prices found in an entity's exchange transactions. This is typically referred to, as Arnold W. Johnson points out, as the historical cost basis of accounting (Grady, p. 439). In this way, diverse things are recorded in terms of a common denominator (Paton and Littleton, p. 12; AAA, p. 2; Moonitz, p. 18).

Agreement that the accountant should record exchange transaction prices is well-nigh universal. But the term "historical cost" has limited value in describing such prices. To say that sales are recorded at historical cost is not only inappropriate but may actually

---

[7]William J. Vatter, "Postulates and Principles," *Journal of Accounting Research,* Vol. 1, No. 2 (Autumn 1963), pp. 188–190; Louis Goldberg, *An Inquiry into the Nature of Accounting* (American Accounting Association, 1965), pp. 100–101.

be misleading. The terms "price-aggregates" or "measured consideration" are more truly descriptive. And they do not becloud the fact that the accountant is concerned with the service potential of goods and services and not simply their cost (Paton and Littleton, p. 13).

Moonitz (p. 52) has five postulates relating to accounting data. Postulate A-1 contains the observation that quantitative data are useful in making rational economic decisions. Postulate A-2 holds that goods and services are usually exchanged rather than consumed by their producer, while Postulate A-5 notes that money is the common denominator in which measurements of goods and services (including labor, natural resources, and capital) are expressed. Postulate B-2 holds that accounting data are based on past, present, or future exchange prices. These four postulates form the basis for the imperative contained in Postulate C-4 that "accounting reports should be based on a stable unit."

The three A postulates describe the environment in which accounting for business is undertaken in our society. Postulate B-2 accurately describes existing practice in that the accounts usually do contain market prices or allocations of them, although it does not specify whether past, present, or future exchange prices are to be recorded (this is dictated at least in part by the accounting requirements of objectivity and realization). Nor does it hold that the entity must be, or expect to be, a party to the transaction before recording its exchange price.

For years the accountant assumed the dollar to be a stable unit of measure (Paton, p. 488; Paton and Littleton, p. 23). In present practice, changes in the purchasing power of the dollar are considered too insignificant to require adjustment. Because he believes this assumption is also invalid, Grady (p. 370) refuses to use the common denominator argument to explain the practice of recording exchange prices. Without adjustment for changes in the value of the dollar, such prices are not common expressions. His position calls for the reporting of the effects of price level changes upon financial statements, and since this embraces use of a constant unit of measure it is similar to Moonitz's Postulate C-4.

Why does the accountant accept the bargained prices in exchange transactions as his basic data? In addition to the common denominator argument, three reasons exist: (1) Many of the changes in an entity's resources and claims to resources are readily discernible in exchange transactions. (2) An exchange price is prima facie evidence of the money value of the goods and services exchanged (AAA, p. 3). (3) There is no reasonable alternative. Unless he records exchange prices, the accountant would have to "second guess" management and find independently a value to attach to the goods and services exchanged and held. The precariousness of his position should be obvious, especially since he possesses no special skill as an appraiser.

Should exchange transaction prices be the basic data of accounting? The answer is a qualified yes. Much of the economic activity of an entity can be properly quantified in this manner, provided that the prices resulted from arm's-length bargaining between independent entities, the parties to the exchange acted rationally, and sufficient market activity exists to give credence to the assumption that the prices are representative (Moonitz, p. 29). But some significant changes, such as increases in asset values, may go unrecognized for years until an exchange takes place. This limitation is dealt with in Chapter 4.

CONSISTENCY BETWEEN PERIODS FOR THE SAME ENTITY

The consistency concept holds that the accounting practices and procedures of a *specific entity* should be consistently applied *through time*. If not, this fact must be disclosed and sufficient information presented to enable a user to compare successive financial statements.

The importance of the requirement of consistency has long been recognized (AAA, p. 9; Sanders, Hatfield, and Moore, p. 113; Theory Statement, p. 18; Moonitz, p. 43). But in one deductive model of accounting theory, consistency is a constraint, not a postulate, encountered in attempting to apply the model and resulting from the uncertainty surrounding economic activity (Hendriksen, p. 80).

Because different accounting practices may be employed in a variety of settings, the circumstances in which the consistency concept is not considered applicable should be detailed. The concept does not require the following: (1) All entities within a given industry to use the same accounting practices. (2) An entity to refrain from discarding one practice in favor of another which, in its opinion, more clearly depicts the underlying circumstances. (3) Consistent practices within an entity in a time period—for example, an entity may use both the LIFO and FIFO inventory methods for different inventories in the same accounting period. (4) Consistency between accounting statements — the balance sheet may show accounts receivable arising from installment sales (accrual basis) while the income statement shows only revenues collected (cash basis). (5) That the accounting practices adopted be the most appropriate ones for the measurement of an entity's activities or position, although several dissenters argue that it should (Moonitz, p. 43; Theory Statement, p. 17).

And it has been suggested that the consistency concept should be related to basic notions such as the nature of business income, terminology, and even to the form of accounting reports (Theory Statement, p. 18).

Consistency is desired so that differences revealed in an analysis of comparative data will reflect actual changes in underlying conditions. For example, an entity might report earnings per share of $4.06 one year and $4.66 the following year. But if the increase of $.60 were caused solely by a change to a policy of capitalizing rather than expensing research costs when incurred, the change is not "real" and may be misleading. Since the data are not comparable, the difference is not truly descriptive and useful.

The consistency requirement exists basically because the application of alternative practices may yield vastly divergent results. These practices exist because the accountant lacks the means for demonstrating the superiority of one practice over another. And this inability stems directly from the inherent uncertainty which characterizes measurements of economic activity.[8] For this reason, the consistency concept will probably never be discarded.

DIVERSITY IN ACCOUNTING AMONG INDEPENDENT ENTITIES

The highly controversial question of diversity versus uniformity is considered in a later chapter. Consequently, attention is drawn here only to the existence of considerable disagreement with the position that diversity is, in effect, a fact of life (Grady, p. 33). Many, including a number of Grady's advisory committee, would argue that diversity is not a basic concept of accounting (Grady, pp. 437–439, 442–443, and 444).[9]

[8]For further discussion, see Chapter 6, *infra.*

[9]See also Robert N. Anthony's review of Grady's Inventory, *The Accounting Review,* Vol. 41 (January 1966), p. 195.

CONSERVATISM

Conservatism is the quality of judgment, to be exercised in the evaluation of business risks, which requires reasonable provisions for possible losses on recorded assets and in the settlement of liabilities. It is the somewhat doubting attitude possessed by the accountant as a counterbalance to the natural optimism of the business executive. Within the scope of generally accepted accounting principles, conservatism embraces the refusal to anticipate income and the requirement that all known or probable liabilities and losses be recorded even though they may not be definitely measurable. In this manner conservatism is closely related to realization. Grady concedes that past, and perhaps current, practices in closely held corporations deliberately understate assets and income. But he argues that such a view of conservatism has no applicability to widely held corporations and misses the entire significance of the concept (pp. 35–36).

But there is much evidence against the contentions that conservatism is solely a question of realization and that the accountant's tendency to lean toward understatement of assets, income, and stockholders' equity has disappeared. Understatement of financial position and income tends to result from the application of many currently accepted practices, including LIFO, cost or market, whichever is lower, and the reporting of intangible assets at $1 or omitting them entirely. And the practicing accountant asserts so strongly that the concept does not justify deliberate understatement that one can only ask: Does he not protest too much? But it probably is true today, as it was in 1939 when Gilman made note of it, that few nonaccountants realize the significance of the accounting concept of conservatism.[10]

The concept of conservatism exists for two main reasons: (1) the uncertainty surrounding the activities the accountant seeks to measure and (2) the lack of objective data, which causes many of his measurements to be tentative. Additionally, in years past when ownership interests were relatively constant, no great damage was done by "playing safe" and understating assets, income, and ownership interest, since all benefits ultimately accrued to the same owners.[11] The influence of creditors from the era in which financial

---

[10]Stephen Gilman, *Accounting Concepts of Profit,* (New York: The Ronald Press Company, 1939), p. 232.

[11]The understatement of financial position of an entity has even received legal approbation; see *Newton v. Birmingham Small Arms Co.,* 2 Ch. 378; 1906 W. N. 146.

statements were used primarily for credit-seeking purposes is unmistakable. Most "conservative" practices also tend to avoid or delay the payment of taxes. And users of present-day financial statements, including bankers and financial analysts, approve "conservative" financial statements.[12]

Should accounting data be conservatively reported? If conservatism is simply an admonition to proceed in a prudent manner, considering all relevant factors, it has a rightful place in accounting (Moonitz, p. 47). It should be rejected if it calls for selecting the lowest value for assets (highest for liabilities), disregarding the modal or most probable value. Choosing the lowest value for an asset can be accepted only if it is the least damaging approach — that is, if all possible values have the same probability of occurrence (Hendriksen, p. 94). A concept of conservatism embracing bias toward understatement must be rejected. To be useful, accounting data must be free of bias (Theory Statement, p. 11). Financial analysts are apparently in the paradoxical position of viewing the diversity in accounting practices with dismay while advocating the presentation of conservative data; differences in the degree of severity in the application of conservatism can destroy comparability as readily as can diverse accounting practices.

Conservatism is not an essential element in a deductive model of accounting theory; a statistical approach is far preferable (Moonitz, pp. 47–48; Hendriksen, p. 94). For example, inventory might be reported at $1,040,000 plus or minus $200,000 on a 95 per cent confidence basis (Theory Statement, p. 65).

The possibility that conservatism (in the sense of understatement) may conflict with disclosure should be readily apparent. Conservatism may also conflict with consistency and with a proper matching of costs with revenue.

DEPENDABILITY OF DATA
THROUGH INTERNAL CONTROL

According to Grady, the dependability of accounting data "is obtained through appropriate measures of internal control." Internal control is defined "as comprising the plan of organization and all of the co-ordinate methods and measures adopted within a business

---

[12]Morton Backer, "Financial Reporting and Security Investment Decisions," *Financial Executive*, Vol. 34 (December 1966), p. 53.

to safe-guard its assets, check the accuracy and reliability of its accounting data, promote operational efficiency, and encourage adherence to prescribed managerial policies" (p. 37).

The dependability of accounting data rests upon more than a high degree of verifiability in the documentary evidence of an entity's transactions with external parties. A system of internal control, operated by qualified personnel, is needed so that internal judgments, such as assignment of costs and revenues to periods, will reflect relevant facts and circumstances.

This concept of dependability embraces the widely discussed, but often poorly defined, concept of objectivity. As stated in Moonitz's Postulate C-2 (p. 50), the objectivity concept requires that "changes in assets and the related effects . . . should not be given formal recognition in the accounts" until they can be objectively measured. Accounting data are objectively measurable when they are supported by objective evidence — that is, evidence which can be verified by a competent investigator (Moonitz, p. 42) or impersonal or external evidence, not personal opinion (Paton and Littleton, p. 19).

In these views of objectivity, accounting data exist independently of the accountant and his measurement process. While this may be appropriate for certain measurements (for example, the closing market price of a security on a given date on a given exchange), other measurements (such as the annual net income of an entity), cannot be obtained independently of the accountant's measurement and judgment processes.[13] Objectivity is therefore more realistically defined as a consensus among observers, not based on the existence of factors external to and independent of those who perceive them.[14]

When defined in this manner, accounting measurements will have varying degrees of objectivity depending upon the object being measured, the degree of specificity in the measurement rules, and the capabilities of those applying the rules. Measures of the cost of a self-constructed asset, for example, may vary somewhat among accountants and may vary even more widely among nonaccountants.

Other accountants include the absence of bias in their definitions

[13] Yuji Ijiri and Robert K. Jaedicke, "Reliability and Objectivity of Accounting Measurements," *The Accounting Review*, Vol. 41 (July 1966), p. 476.

[14] *Ibid.* When defined to mean consensus, the objectivity of a set of measures can be determined through statistical measurement of their *dispersion;* see also Daniel L. MacDonald, "Feasibility Criteria for Accounting Measures," *The Accounting Review*, Vol. 42 (October 1967), pp. 670–673.

of objectivity and assert that accounting data may be biased by the use of an inappropriate measurement method as well as by an absence of verifiable evidence.[15] When defined in this manner, objectivity embraces the evidence supporting a measure, the question of bias in the method selected, and the appropriateness of the measure itself in fulfilling accounting objectives. Grady apparently used the term "dependability" in this broad sense. Some of the accountant's actions can be explained only by acknowledging that he does have certain objectives in mind other than reliance upon verifiable evidence. For example, he consistently rejects market values in excess of cost for securities and inventories even though they may possess a high degree of verifiability. On the other hand, asset amortizations are often based on the flimsiest of verifiable evidence. Unfortunately, these objectives may not be clearly stated.

The narrower of the two definitions of objectivity is preferable, although it should be used in the sense of a consensus and applied to the measure itself rather than to the evidence used to support it. The broader definition lacks precision since it, in effect, embraces the concepts or standards of objectivity (in the narrow sense), freedom from bias, and relevance—three important attributes which give information utility.

An adequate system of internal control will tend to give accounting measurements greater objectivity largely by ensuring that competent personnel have ascertained that prescribed measurement rules have been properly applied. But such a system cannot guarantee that the methods prescribed by management are not biased or that the measurements are relevant to a specific decision.

External users require information possessing a rather high degree of objectivity. This is especially true where parties with opposing interests rely upon the information prepared by one of the parties. Unless such information conforms to an objectivity standard it may be slanted and may for this reason impair the functioning of our economic system. But objectivity is not the primary standard in appraising the utility of accounting information; relevance is (Theory Statement, p. 9).

Certain guides to accounting action, such as realization, seem definitely related to the concept of dependability of data through

[15] Paul E. Fertig, "Current Values and Index Numbers: The Problem of Objectivity," *Research in Accounting Measurement,* Robert K. Jaedicke, Yuji Ijiri, and Oswald Nielsen, eds., (Evanston, Ill.: American Accounting Association, 1966), pp. 137–149.

internal control. But the dependability of accounting data is more nearly an objective than a basic concept of accounting. "One cannot postulate objectivity; it must be maintained by methodology . . . "[16] And so it is with dependability.

In a somewhat similar vein, it can be argued that objectivity is not a postulate. Although Moonitz includes it as one of his C postulates, he refers to them as imperatives and defines them as goals or objectives (p. 38). Hendriksen argues that, in a deductive model, objectivity is more an environmental constraint resulting from uncertainty in the application of logically deduced accounting principles.

MATERIALITY

That accountants should concern themselves only with material matters is a notion permeating all of accounting. The *Accounting Research Bulletins* are claimed to be applicable only to material items;[17] the APB Opinions are implicitly applicable to material items since they are explicitly not applicable to immaterial items;[18] and Rule 1.02 of the SEC's *Regulation S-X* states the Commission's requirement on the disclosure of material information.

The fundamental meaning of materiality is that one need not be concerned with unimportant things. Grady (p. 40) provides the following more complete definition (which he attributes to Dohr):

A statement, fact, or item is material, if giving full consideration to the surrounding circumstances, as they exist at the time, it is of such a nature that its disclosure, or the method of treating it, would be likely to influence or to "make a difference" in the judgment or conduct of a reasonable person. The same tests apply to such words as significant, consequential, or important.

This definition is general and could apply equally well to sociology. Another definition, while running along similar lines, is more closely related to accounting in that it substitutes the fiction of "an informed investor" for Grady's reasonable person (AAA, p. 8).

[16]Vatter, *op. cit.*, p. 190.

[17]*Accounting Research and Terminology Bulletins,* Final Edition (New York: American Institute of Certified Public Accountants, 1961), p. 9.

[18] Accounting Principles Board, "Accounting for the Investment Credit," *Opinion No. 2* (New York: American Institute of Certified Public Accountants, 1962), p. 9, or see any subsequent opinion.

The concept of materiality does not relate solely to dollar amounts reported, it also relates to changes in such dollar amounts, to corrections of prior periods' data, to the manner in which disclosure is made, as well as to nonquantifiable statements of fact and descriptions of quantified data. Its application largely involves exercising judgment rather than following precise rules.[19]

Materiality exists largely for economic reasons. It deters expending time and resources on inconsequential items or matters. And while not a postulate of accounting, it may be a constraint since it restricts the reporting of insignificant details while calling for the reporting of material information (Hendriksen, p. 93).

The requirement that material items be separately disclosed has helped detect biased reporting. One study shows the existence of a tendency to report material extraordinary items with credit balances in the income statement while carrying losses and other debit items to the statement of retained earnings.[20] *Opinion No. 9* attempts to resolve this problem by requiring the reporting of all extraordinary items in the income statement, except corrections of prior periods' data.[21]

Numerous problems exist because of the lack of clear-cut guides for applying the concept. Should the materiality of an item be determined by relating it to net income, normal net income, sales, balance sheet footings, or simply from the nature of the item itself? Data otherwise comparable may be rendered noncomparable due to different notions of materiality. An item deemed immaterial in one year, as determined by a reference to net income, may be deemed material the next year simply because net income fell. The loss of an immaterial amount of cash may be a material fact if it indicates a breakdown in the system of internal control.

Materiality is not a basic postulate in a deductive model of accounting theory (Moonitz, pp. 46–47). A deductive model, which seeks to set standards from which deviations may be measured, cannot fulfill this function if an indeterminable allowance for deviations is built into the standard.

---

[19] An exception exists in SEC practice; see Rule 1.02 of *Regulation S-X* for the 15 per cent rule employed in defining a significant subsidiary.

[20] Leopold A. Bernstein, "The Concept of Materiality," *The Accounting Review,* Vol. 42 (January 1967), p. 87.

[21] Accounting Principles Board, "Reporting the Results of Operations," *Opinion No. 9* (New York: American Institute of Certified Public Accountants, 1966), pp. 112–113.

TIMELINESS IN FINANCIAL REPORTING REQUIRES ESTIMATES

In his discussion of this topic, Grady (p. 41) deals only with the time period aspect of the timeliness of information. Consequently, attention is directed first to the idea embraced in Moonitz's Postulate A-4 (p. 52) that "economic activity is carried on during specifiable periods of time." But the concept does not explicitly include what is essentially an imperative also contained in Postulate A-4 that reports on such activity must identify the time period involved.

Grady recognizes that reporting in terms of time periods is necessary to provide timely information, but he does not specifically deal with the length of the accounting period. That the accounting period should be a year undoubtedly is a reflection of natural phenomena and our agricultural heritage. Moonitz argues that there is no fundamental significance to the year as the accounting period other than comparability through time (pp. 16–17).

Grady implicitly recognizes, as have many others, that the foundation for the accrual basis of accounting lies in the fact that the events comprising economic activity do not fall neatly into accounting periods of prescribed length (Moonitz, p. 33; Paton and Littleton, pp. 9–10, 22; Sanders, Hatfield, and Moore, p. 113; AAA, p. 5). As a result, many accounting measurements will necessarily involve allocations and accruals based upon estimates and judgment. Grady also implies that the more timely the information, the greater its tentativeness — another of the Moonitz postulates:

> Postulate B-4. Tentativeness. (Related to A-4). The results of operations for relatively short periods of time are tentative whenever allocations between past, present, and future periods are required (Moonitz, p. 52).

Whenever accounting data are based on estimates and judgment, hindsight may reveal actual differences. Grady suggests that the bulk of these differences should be absorbed in subsequent periods' operations unless the amounts are large enough to distort periodic income.[22] He believes that a strong argument exists for not calling these differences errors if the estimates were based upon rational analysis and best judgment — depreciation revisions are examples.

The unquestioned need for information useful in decision making in our complex, fast-moving economy demands periodic financial

[22] Cf. *ibid.*

reporting. One of the attributes of such useful information is its time-liness, which depends in part upon the length of the time interval for which it is accumulated. Thus, information on a business entity for a single ten-year period would be almost worthless to a person currently facing a decision to buy or sell shares of stock in the entity.

On the other hand, financial data for shorter periods — a month, a quarter, or even a year — may be quite timely but so tentative that they lack utility. This tentativeness results from the use of estimates, which is the source of many problems. In addition, the accountant faces the question, similar to the relevance versus objectivity issue, of how much objectivity should be sacrificed to secure greater time-liness. Typically, he chooses the more objective data, as exemplified by his refusal to recognize accretion on timber until it is cut (Moonitz, pp. 33–34).

Speed of reporting is the other aspect of the timeliness of infor-mation; Grady does not deal with this, and it is apparently ignored by all but systems designers. Delay in reporting information may sharply reduce its utility. Information first available in 1968 of an entity's earnings per share for 1966 would be of little value in decid-ing in 1968 whether to purchase stock in that entity. Delay in report-ing also has a bearing upon tentativeness and materiality because carefully developed financial reports take longer to prepare and also reduce the areas requiring estimates. In the future, as accountants devote more attention to systems design and to communication and information theory, they will be more likely to consider speed of re-porting as an aspect of accounting theory.

Hendriksen (pp. 88–90) accepts the idea of time periods as a basic postulate in his deductive model but considers tentativeness an environmental constraint occasioned by uncertainty.

COMPARATIVE SUMMARY

Nine of the ten concepts considered basic to an inventory of accounting principles have been discussed and compared with the postulates of several deductive models of accounting theory. As might have been expected, differences exist not only because of per-sonal beliefs and biases but because of differences in approach. For example, the concepts presented by Grady are considered basic to those accounting principles currently considered acceptable. The basic postulates presented by Moonitz, on the other hand, were derived primarily as a foundation for expressing what accounting principles *ought* to be.

Grady (pp. 23–24) further argues that his concepts were derived by observing how a business meets its accountabilities. These concepts "may be justified as providing qualities of usefulness and dependability to accounting information or as setting forth limitations in the financial statements produced by the accounting process." Rather than observations of accounting actions, postulates are defined as observations of the environment in which accounting is to function, especially of the economic activity which accounting is to measure and report upon.

Yet, because either concepts or postulates are considered necessary when attempting to discover or formulate the principles of accounting, a certain amount of similarity is to be expected. This similarity can readily be seen as extending to the ideas of entity, continuity, consistency, periodicity, and tentativeness, although it can be argued that consistency is to be maintained rather than postulated. And from the discussions presented and by implication, the concept of monetary expression in the accounts can be seen to embrace the postulates of quantification, exchange, money unit of measure, and stability of the unit of measure.

Some may question whether stability of the unit of measure is a postulate since it states what ought to be rather than describing the environment. Similarly, dependability of data through internal control and objectivity seem more nearly objectives of accounting than concepts and postulates. And while the concepts of diversity, conservatism, and materiality certainly influence accounting practice, it is questionable that they belong in any model of accounting theory as concepts or postulates.

Grady considers the following two postulates to be generally accepted principles rather than basic concepts:

Postulate B-1. Financial Statements. (Related to A-1). The results of the accounting process are expressed in a set of fundamentally related financial statements which articulate with each other and rest upon the same underlying data.

Postulate C-5. Disclosure. Accounting reports should disclose that which is necessary to make them not misleading (Moonitz, pp. 52–53).

Hendriksen (pp. 85–86) includes all of the A postulates (quantification, exchange, entities, time period, and unit of measure) and Postulates B-2, B-3, and C-1 (market prices, entities, continuity) as the environmental postulates in his model. Postulates B-4, C-2, C-3, and C-4 (tentativeness, objectivity, consistency, and stable unit) and possibly conservatism and materiality are environmental constraints resulting from uncertainty. Postulate C-5 (disclosure) is an objective of accounting, while Postulate B-1 (financial statements) is part of the accounting framework along with ledgers, journals, and accounts.

Many would cite realization, among other ideas considered fundamental in accounting, as a basic concept (AAA, p. 3; Sanders, Hatfield, and Moore, p. 114).[23] Grady (p. 36) considers it a part of the broader concept of conservatism. And while realization and objectivity seem closely related, neither Moonitz nor Hendriksen considers it a postulate of accounting. Realization is explored in depth in a later chapter.

Paton and Littleton (pp. 13–18) cite the ideas that costs attach (they can be allocated and regrouped into significant groups) and effort and accomplishment (the matching notion) as basic accounting concepts. These are certainly fundamental to accounting and will be dealt with later. And while perhaps not a basic concept, an input-output system (double-entry bookkeeping with its convention of debit and credit) is universally accepted.

While other ideas have been advanced as basic concepts of accounting, none has received support comparable to that accorded the concepts presented in this chapter.

QUESTIONS

1. Which of the various approaches to accounting theory discussed in Chapter 1 is employed by Grady in *ARS No. 7*? Explain.

2. Explain carefully the meaning of the term "basic concept" as it is used in *ARS No. 7*.

3. (a) In what respects do basic concepts differ from basic postulates? (b) Why do they differ?

4. Of the many ideas discussed in this chapter and referred to as assumptions, concepts, and postulates, which seem truly basic to the theory of accounting? Explain.

[23]See also Study Group on Business Income, *Changing Concepts of Business Income* (New York: The Macmillan Company, 1952), pp. 19ff.; Anthony, *op. cit.*, p. 195.

5. Which of the concepts in *ARS No. 7* tend to set forth limitations in the financial statements produced by the accounting process? Explain.

6. Is the concept of rational action as basic to accounting as conservatism or consistency? Discuss.

7. In accounting for a business entity, does the accountant assume that the entity has a goal of profit maximization? Is a profit motive assumed? Explain.

8. Does the accounting function involve the selection of certain data from a vast amount of existing data or does it actually embrace the creation of additional data? Explain.

9. Must the basic concepts of accounting be unique to accounting—that is, not applicable to or found in other disciplines? Why or why not?

10. Indicate how the entity concept provides a foundation for a proposition used as a guide to accounting action.

11. What criteria should be employed in determining the boundaries of an entity?

12. Does the accountant's failure to record the right to use leased property violate the concept of "A society and government structure honoring private property rights"? Explain.

13. If continuity were open to inquiry rather than an assumption, who should decide whether financial statements are to be based upon the assumption of continuity? Why?

14. With several examples, show that the appropriate concept of the entity depends upon the point of view of the different users of accounting data.

15. Consider the typical bases of valuation of assets in accounting. Although all are expressed in dollar amounts, are they all reported in terms of a common denominator? Explain.

16. Describe briefly the evolution of the monetary postulate or concept of accounting.

17. Is consistency a concept, constraint, or objective in a model of accounting theory? Explain.

18. According to *ARS No. 7*, disclosure is a principle of and conservatism a basic concept of accounting. How might it be maintained that these two positions are inconsistent and contradictory?

19. Reconcile the concept of "dependability of data through internal control" with the more familiar concept of objectivity.

20. Explain why materiality should not be included in a model of accounting theory.

21. (a) Explain why the timeliness and conclusiveness (objectivity) of information are often in conflict. (b) In which direction does the accountant tend to resolve this conflict? Illustrate.

22. (a) What is the approach to accounting theory implied in the statement of postulates or concepts as starting propositions? (b) What are the major deficiencies in this approach?

23. It has been argued that any account balance of more than $1 million is a material amount in financial reporting and should be separately disclosed. State whether you agree with this position and why.

4

INCOME
CONCEPTS

Since the early 1930s the determination of periodic net income has been the acknowledged primary function of the accountant. Income determination reached this position of primacy largely because measurements of income were used for an expanding number of purposes. Although some question how well they have served, such measurements have been used for a number of purposes, among them: (1) to appraise the effectiveness of management in using resources; (2) as a basis for predicting future incomes, especially by present and prospective stockholders; (3) management's evaluation of past decisions in order to improve decision making; (4) as a basis for taxation; (5) as a guide to dividend policy; (6) as a basis for price and rate regulation; (7) in determining credit worthiness; (8) in collective bargaining between labor and management; and (9) as a basis in formulating broad social policies.

One school of thought holds that future progress in accounting theory depends upon agreement on a concept of income and suggests that the proper approach is to make accounting measurements of income conform more closely with economic income.[1] A second group, as exemplified by the American Accounting Association committees which prepared Supplementary Statement No. 1 to the Association's 1957 Revision and *A Statement of Basic Accounting Theory,* advocates the reporting of multiple measurements of income and other financial data. A third group believes that it is impossible to get the income measurements needed and, as a result, the determination of periodic net income will be superseded by other measures such as the contribution concept, cash flow, and funds flow.[2] A part of this dissatisfaction with the income

[1] G. Edward Philips, "The Accretion Concept of Income," *The Accounting Review,* Vol. 38 (January 1963), pp. 14–25.

[2] David Solomons, "Economic and Accounting Concepts of Income," *The Accounting Review,* Vol. 36 (July 1961), pp. 374–383.

concept probably stems from the wide diversity in measurements of income resulting from the application of many alternative accounting procedures.

But in spite of this discontent, income determination has not yet been dislodged from its pedestal, and much of financial accounting today is undertaken with income determination in mind. For this reason, income concepts — psychic, economic, and accounting — are explored in this and the succeeding chapter.

PSYCHIC INCOME

Every individual is motivated by his desires and wants to satisfy them.[3] Satisfying these desires tends to add to an individual's sense of well being. And the action taken to satisfy them produces psychic income — the ideal concept of income.[4] But an individual's wants and his sense of well being are personal and subjective. They cannot be known by anyone else and cannot be measured. To obtain some degree of objectivity of measurement, noneconomic satisfactions must be excluded from a concept of income. But excluding noneconomic satisfactions sacrifices a substantial degree of reality for objectivity.[5]

ECONOMIC INCOME

When an individual has economic wants, his sense of well being can be improved by goods and services that can be exchanged for money.[6] Goods and services measurable in money terms form the economist's definition of wealth. Because money measurements can be summed to obtain a representation of total wealth, economists prefer wealth to well being as the basis for income measurement. If the bulk of an individual's wants are satisfied by goods and services that can be measured in money, economic income may approximate psychic income.

[3]For a discussion of basic human behavior, see Raymond J. Chambers, *Accounting Evaluation and Economic Behavior* (Englewood Cliffs, N. J.: Prentice-Hall, Inc., 1966), esp. Chap. 1 and 2.

[4]For a further discussion of psychic income, see Norton M. Bedford, *Income Determination Theory: An Accounting Framework* (Reading, Mass.: Addison-Wesley Publishing Company, 1965), pp. 20–23.

[5]Philips, *op. cit.,* p. 16.

[6]Sidney S. Alexander, "Income Measurement in a Dynamic Economy," revised by David Solomons, in W. T. Baxter and Sidney Davidson, *Studies in Accounting Theory* (Homewood, Ill.: Richard D. Irwin, Inc., 1962), p. 137.

Beginning with Adam Smith, many economists have viewed income as existing only after capital has been maintained.[7] Currently, the most commonly accepted definition of economic income is Hicks': "the maximum amount a person can consume during a week and still expect to be as well-off at the end of the week as he was at the beginning."[8] And, from this, a business entity's income is defined as the maximum amount of dividends it can pay in a period and still be as well off at the end as at the beginning of the period. To be equally as well off at these two points means that capital must have been maintained, and this raises the issue of how capital maintenance is to be measured. The most commonly advocated basis is the discounting or capitalization of expected cash receipts; others prefer measurements of the physical quantities or the market values of the resources held. A distinguishing feature of economic income is that it must be measured in real terms; that is, adjustments should be used to eliminate the effects of general price level changes.

Capitalized Net Receipts

The value of the capital invested in any undertaking can be measured by discounting its expected net cash receipts by an appropriate discount rate. Assume, for example, that a firm expects a net cash inflow of $1,000 at the end of each of the next three years, 1971, 1972, and 1973. The $1,000 may be an expectation known with certainty or it may be the average of a possible range of receipts, each weighted by its probability of occurrence. If, in view of alternatives available, the management of the firm would not undertake this investment unless it earns at least 10 per cent (the target rate), the present value of this investment is $2,487.

Of the $1,000 received during the year 1971, $249 is income and is computed as follows:

Cash received	$1,000
Discounted value at end of 1971 of	
two annual expected cash receipts	
of $1,000	1,736
Total value at end of 1971	$2,736
Less: Value at beginning of 1971	2,487
Income for 1971	$ 249

[7]For a discussion of various economic concepts of income, see Emily Chen Chang, "Business Income in Accounting and Economics," *The Accounting Review,* Vol. 37 (October 1962), pp. 638–639.

[8]J. R. Hicks, *Value and Capital* (Oxford: Clarendon Press, 1946), p. 172.

The remainder of the $1,000 received is a return of capital. If the payments are certain; the income for the year can also be computed by multiplying the capitalized value of the investment at the beginning of the year by the discount rate ($2,487 × .10). The $249 is called the subjective income for the year since it represents the change in the subjective value of the firm from the beginning to the end of the year.

Subjective income may be computed before or after the period to which it relates has expired. In its expected sense, it represents the expected change in subjective value between two dates. In its actual sense, it includes expected income as well as unexpected gains and losses.

In the above example, expected subjective income and actual subjective income are the same because expectations were realized and remained unchanged. Assume now that the actual cash received in the first year was $1,500 and that expectations changed so that two future net cash inflows of $1,100 are expected at the end of each of the next two years. The income for 1971 is computed as follows:

Cash received	$1,500
Discounted value at end of 1971 of two annual expected cash receipts of $1,100	1,910
Total value at end of 1971	$3,410
Less: Value at beginning of 1971	2,487
Income for 1971	$ 923

This $923 actually consists of several elements:

Expected subjective income ($2,487 × .10)	$ 249
Unexpected cash receipt in 1971 ($1,500 − $1,000)	500
Increase in subjective value at end of 1971 ($1,910 − $1,736)	174
	$ 923

Economists tend to disagree about whether the $923 is income for 1971 in its entirety. Because expectations for the year were exceeded and future expectations changed, the beginning value of $2,487 was not the actual subjective value of the firm at the beginning of the year. Consequently, it is argued that a part of the $923 is more properly viewed as a correction of prior-year incomes than as an element of current income.

But, as illustrated above, subjective income is an all-inclusive income concept. If actually applied in a manufacturing company, subjective income would undoubtedly include (1) income realized from delivery and sale of product; (2) unrealized income from increases in value resulting from the production of goods not yet sold; (3) realized gains and losses of an unexpected, windfall nature; and (4) unrealized changes in capitalized value resulting from either internal (changes in efficiency) or external (changes in demand) factors.

LIMITATIONS. The major limitation of the subjective income concept is that, as a practical matter, it cannot be rendered operational because it is so heavily based on unverifiable, subjective expectations. And because it is so based, income can vary widely simply by changing the estimates of the amounts or the periods of cash flow expected or by varying the discount rate. Even if there is no intent to mislead, bias is apt to be present simply because of the difficulty of distinguishing between emotional opinion and realistic estimates of future receipts.[9]

As a further limitation, there is no need to compute subjective income when cash flows can be predicted with certainty since subjective income is already known. The present value of the expected cash flows is the subjective value of the firm; income is simply this value at the beginning of the period multiplied by the discount rate. And the changes in expectations that accompany uncertainty will, as already noted, require revisions of prior periods' incomes, thus introducing questions about how these are to be treated consistently.[10]

The necessity of computing periodic income when cash flows are known may also be questioned. It has been established, at least in theory, that many users of financial information need projections of cash flow and little else in order to make intelligent decisions. Measurements of income are used solely as a basis for predicting cash flows.[11]

[9] Bedford, *op. cit.*, p. 27.
[10] Eldon S. Hendriksen, *Accounting Theory* (Homewood, Ill.: Richard D. Irwin, Inc., 1965), p. 107.
[11] Committee to Prepare a Statement of Basic Accounting Theory, *A Statement of Basic Accounting Theory* (Evanston, Ill.: American Accounting Association, 1966), p. 23 fn.

Finally, subjective income, unless supplemented by data revealing the sources of income, does not provide information (1) to indicate whether capital was maintained by planned action or by luck, (2) to appraise managerial effectiveness in using resources, and (3) to serve as a basis for prediction.

Yet, in spite of its many limitations, the subjective income model is useful as a standard to appraise managerial efficiency in planning and predicting future economic activity.[12] Businessmen probably do seek to maximize their subjective values, which they expect to convert into market values. And uncertain estimates of future receipts are used to value property, especially in making decisions on capital expenditures.[13]

Market Values

Economists and accountants have supported measuring income as the change in the total of the current selling prices of the net assets, as adjusted for capital changes.[14] Some support the use of market values on the grounds that they provide the best objective approximations to the subjective values considered ideal.[15] On the other hand, market values are themselves considered the ideal measures of value in computing income. Income is considered an accretion to economic power, and it is maintained that economic power does not exist without market values.[16] The amount by which the present value of an asset's future receipts exceeds its market value cannot be used to acquire goods and services until the asset's market value rises or the receipts are realized.

But the subjective value of an asset (or an entity) will be greater than or equal to its market value or it will be sold. And, if greater, the difference exists because the market does not share the firm's expectations. To the extent that the firm's expectations are correct

---

[12] Bedford, *op. cit.*, p. 28.

[13] Solomons, *op. cit.*, p. 379.

[14] Among the economists, see Edgar O. Edwards and Phillip W. Bell, *The Theory and Measurement of Business Income* (Berkeley and Los Angeles: The University of California Press, 1961), p. 25, and supporting references cited there. Others are Robert M. Haig, Henry C. Simons, and Richard A. Musgrave, as cited in Philips, *op. cit.*, p. 20. Accountants supporting the use of market values are Philips, *op. cit.*, and Chambers, *op. cit.*

[15] Alexander, *op. cit.*; also, see references cited in Edwards and Bell, *op. cit.*, fn. p. 25.

[16] Philips, *op. cit.*, p. 17. It should be noted here that Philips and Chambers regard market values as the ideal measures, while Edwards and Bell suggest that they provide only an ideal short-run concept of profit (see page 25).

and are subsequently reflected in market values, it can be urged that economic power does exist before it appears in market values.[17]

DEFICIENCIES. Using market values to measure income has several other deficiencies. Since market values are not available for many assets, such assets are included at zero value when income is computed. Yet if the assets were known to be available, willing buyers could possibly be found. A second objection is that the total of the market values obtainable for the individual assets of a plant, division, or firm may not sum to the price a willing buyer would pay for the entire unit.[18] The difference represents an intangible value attaching to and inseparable from a given group of assets. Such values are ignored in the market value approach even though they often bulk relatively large.

It is also argued that the valuation of individual assets at market values — essentially at liquidation values — is not appropriate for a going concern where production processes extend beyond the lives of various assets used in the processes.[19] Since the assets will be replaced, replacement prices, not selling prices, are relevant. In a similar vein, reporting current selling prices to stockholders may be inappropriate since stockholders have little practical power to bring about the termination of the firm or any part of its operations. The entity will, because of management's desire, continue operating.

Although the lack of objectivity is often cited as the reason why market values are not widely employed in accounting, the actual reason lies in a concept of income based upon realization, as will be discussed later. Market values generally reflect replacement prices when property is valued at cost or market, whichever is lower. When used as measures of net realizable values, they represent approximations of subjective value.

ACCOUNTING INCOME

Like economists, accountants do not agree on a single concept of income. While there is general agreement that income is the excess

---

[17]Kenneth W. Lemke, "Asset Valuation and Income Theory," *The Accounting Review*, Vol. 41 (January 1966), p. 39.

[18]Kermit Larson and R. W. Schattke, "Current Cash Equivalent, Additivity, and Financial Action," *The Accounting Review*, Vol. 41 (October 1966), pp. 637–640. This is, of course, an extension of the long-held notion that the value of a going concern may be more than the sum of the value of its recorded parts.

[19]Edwards and Bell, *op. cit.*, pp. 100–101.

of revenues over expenses and that it is to be measured at least originally on transaction-based data, disagreement and controversy surround further specification. And a close examination reveals that the accounting concept of income actually embraces notions abstracted from several income concepts.

The Transactions Approach

Under the transactions approach, revenues and expenses are recorded as changes in assets and equities become evident as a result of an entity's transactions. The term "transaction" is virtually a primitive undefined term in accounting. It is broadly interpreted to include most exchanges with outsiders and certain internal events, such as the transfer of materials from the storeroom to a production center. But certain exchanges with outsiders — leases, for example — are not considered transactions.

ADVANTAGES.   Considerable useful information, not normally found in the balance-sheet approach, is or can be accumulated under the transactions approach to income measurement. This includes (1) total gross revenues as well as revenues by product lines or divisions, (2) income classified as to sources (operating versus nonoperating), (3) income by product lines or divisions, and (4) a recorded guide to the inventorying of assets and liabilities at the end of the period. And since the rights and obligations of an entity virtually require the recording of transactions with outsiders, the information recorded lends itself to an economical determination of income.

CAPITAL MAINTENANCE AND THE TRANSACTIONS APPROACH. Standing alone, the transactions approach yields an incomplete determination of income. Certain changes, such as the expiration of the service potential of plant assets, are not reflected in transactions, at least not until the asset is disposed of. Consequently, the measurement of income in practice involves a combination of the transactions and balance-sheet approaches. The following table synthesizes the notions that income is the excess of revenues over related expenses and that income cannot exist until capital is maintained:[20]

---

[20]Donald A. Corbin, "The Revolution in Accounting," *The Accounting Review*, Vol. 37 (October 1962), p. 628.

	Assets −	Liabili- ties	Owners' Equity = (Net Assets)	Income Statement
Balance, January 1	$100	$40	$60	
Revenues	+20		+20	$20
Related expenses	−10	+3	−13	−13
Balance, December 31	$110	$43	$67	$ 7

Assuming the above amounts to represent thousands of dollars, the net income is $7,000 and can be determined by subtracting $13,000 of related expenses from the $20,000 of revenues, or by deducting the beginning owners' equity of $60,000 from the ending equity of $67,000. The two approaches will always yield the same amount of net income if the same basis of valuation is employed and if capital changes and dividends are taken into account. A proprietary view of income taxes and interest charges must also be taken — that is, they must be viewed as expenses.

If the terms "revenues" and "related expenses" are defined broadly enough to include the recognition of changes not reflected in transactions, a number of different bases of valuation could be employed in the above model and in actual practice. But the typical approach is to include only transaction-based data (usually described as historical costs) and certain other data asserted to be logical extensions of the recorded transactions. The accrual of interest is an example.

THE MONEY INVESTMENT CONCEPT OF CAPITAL.   Reliance upon the notion that realization occurs at the time of sale generally, but not always, prohibits the recording of values higher than cost until an exchange occurs. But the use of values lower than cost is widely accepted. And, at the present time, the effects upon accounting measurements of changes in the value of the dollar are largely ignored. From these guiding propositions, it follows that the capital to be maintained in the determination of income is measured initially, at least, in terms of the actual monetary units invested. Although often described as a historical cost basis, exceptions are sufficiently numerous to rule out any brief, technically accurate description. In other words, the actual approach to measuring capital literally involves a rather complete understanding of existing accounting practices.

ECONOMISTS' CRITICISMS.   Although the accounting concepts of income are explored in depth later, economists' major criticisms of them can be noted here. (1) Because changes in asset values are not usually recorded until the assets are sold, capital gains and losses are not likely to be recognized in the periods in which they occur. For example, the income of any given period probably includes gains of prior periods on assets sold during the current period while excluding unrealized gains on assets not sold in the current period. (2) Capital gains and losses are mixed, through depreciation charges based on historical cost, with operating income when the assets to which they relate are used in operations rather than sold. (3) Since the effects of price level changes are ignored, reported income includes a fictional element, and real (in the sense of price level adjusted) owners' equity is not reported in the balance sheet.[21]

Accounting Income and Changing Price Levels

As noted in Chapter 2, the possible effects of changing price levels upon accounting measurements have long been discussed in the literature of accounting. As a result of the post-World War II inflation in the United States, the Accounting Principles Board in 1961 concluded that it was unrealistic for accountants to assume that fluctuations in the value of the dollar may be ignored; the Board authorized a research project to delve into the problem.[22] Based on actual price level adjustments and opinions of practitioners, the resulting research report suggested that, if the degree of inflation in the United States increased materially, the number of supplementary financial statements adjusted for price level changes would increase substantially.[23] Consequently, it is safe to conclude that substantial numbers of accountants subscribe to the notion that income cannot emerge until money capital, adjusted for general price level changes, is maintained. Capital so measured may be described as a real historic cost or a purchasing power concept of capital.

THE PURCHASING POWER CONCEPT. The purchasing power of

[21] Edwards and Bell, op. cit., pp. 10–11.

[22] As quoted in the resulting report; see Staff of the Accounting Research Division, "Reporting the Financial Effects of Price-Level Changes," Accounting Research Study No. 6 (New York: American Institute of Certified Public Accountants, 1963), p. 1.

[23] Ibid., especially Appendices D and E; see also the comments of Russell Morrison on pages 250–251.

the dollar (or any monetary unit) is simply its ability to command goods and services. And its value for such purposes fluctuates inversely with the general level of prices. For example, if over a certain period prices in general double (an appropriate index rises from, say, 124 to 248), the purchasing power of the dollar is halved. That is, it now possesses the power to command goods and services which previously could have been acquired for 50 cents—thus, the source of the expression "a fifty-cent dollar."

The basic purpose of accounting is to describe economic activity through words and numbers. But accurate description is not possible if the unadjusted measuring unit varies through time. Apparent changes may not be real. For example, over a ten-year period sales may have increased 50 per cent. If prices charged for sales have increased 60 per cent in keeping with the general level of prices, the actual physical volume of goods shipped has declined. Or suppose that a man invested $100,000 in some real estate and sold it some years later for $175,000. On the surface he has a gain of $75,000. But if the general level of prices has doubled, he actually has a purchasing power loss, in current dollars, of $25,000, ignoring the fact that the gain is probably taxable income. That is, in order to maintain his capital in terms of purchasing power, he should have received a sufficient number of year-of-sale dollars so that, after deducting the taxes to be paid, he has $200,000 left, since 200,000 year-of-sale dollars have the same purchasing power as 100,000 year-of-purchase dollars.

It should be obvious that the greater the degree of price change, the greater the probability that measurements through time are of questionable validity and utility. Comparisons of unadjusted data from different time periods are completely worthless, if not actually deceiving, when inflation runs rampant as it did in Germany when an index of the cost of living rose from a 1913 level of one to a 1923 high of 1,535 billion.[24] Such changes should make it clear that there are no sound theoretical arguments against adjusting for price level changes. There are, of course, valid arguments based on practical grounds, such as materiality.

AN EXTENDED ILLUSTRATION.   To serve as a basis for an extended

---

[24]Constantino Bresciani-Turroni, *The Economics of Inflation* (London: George Allen and Unwin, Ltd., 1953), pp. 35–36.

illustration of price level adjustments, financial statements for an
assumed company are presented below.

BALANCE SHEETS

		December 31	
Assets		1968	1969
Cash		$ 20,000	$ 10,000
Inventory		20,000	40,000
Plant assets		$100,000	$100,000
Allowance for depreciation		36,000	40,000
Net		$ 64,000	$ 60,000
Land		48,000	48,000
Total assets		$152,000	$158,000
Equities			
Accounts payable		$ 8,000	$ 8,000
Bonds payable		40,000	40,000
Capital stock		100,000	100,000
Retained earnings		4,000	10,000
Total equities		$152,000	$158,000

INCOME STATEMENT FOR YEAR ENDED DECEMBER 31, 1969

Sales		$200,000
Cost of goods sold:		
Inventory, December 31, 1968	$ 20,000	
Purchases	160,000	
	$180,000	
Inventory, December 31, 1969	40,000	140,000
Gross margin		$ 60,000
Depreciation	$ 4,000	
Other expenses and taxes	46,000	50,000
Net income		$ 10,000
Dividends		4,000
Increase in retained earnings		$ 6,000
Retained earnings, December 31, 1968		4,000
Retained earnings, December 31, 1969		$ 10,000

THE BALANCE-SHEET APPROACH TO INCOME DETERMINATION. The
above comparative balance sheets are repeated below with all dollar amounts expressed in terms of December 31, 1969, price levels.
These adjusted amounts are based on the assumptions (1) that an
appropriate index of prices stood at 54 when the land and plant
assets were acquired and when the capital stock was issued, (2)
that this same index stood at 100 on December 31, 1968, and at

108 on December 31, 1969, and (3) that the respective year-end inventories were acquired when the index stood at 98 and 106 and are accounted for on a FIFO basis.

The adjustment of the nonmonetary items consists simply of multiplying their recorded amounts by a ratio whose numerator is the current price index and whose denominator is the index at time of acquisition or issuance. Thus, the equivalent purchasing power on December 31, 1969, to the $48,000 original historical cost of the land is $96,000 ($48,000 × 108/54) because prices have doubled since acquisition. And the $96,000 is the *cost* of the land, *not its current value* — which may be substantially greater, expressed in current purchasing-power equivalents. This adjustment should never be characterized as a write-up (an anathema in accounting practice). It is cost in the truest sense of an economic sacrifice. Only the effects of fluctuations in the unit of measure have been eliminated.

BALANCE SHEETS ADJUSTED TO DECEMBER 31, 1969, PRICES

Assets	1968	1969
Cash	$ 21,600	$ 10,000
Inventory	22,040	40,755
Plant assets	$200,000	$200,000
Allowance for depreciation	72,000	80,000
Net	$128,000	$120,000
Land	96,000	96,000
Total assets	$267,640	$266,755

Equities		
Accounts payable	$ 8,640	$ 8,000
Bonds payable	43,200	40,000
Capital stock	200,000	200,000
Retained earnings	15,800	18,755
Total equities	$267,640	$266,755

Plant assets, the allowance for depreciation, and capital stock are all similarly adjusted through the same multiplier. The December 31, 1968, inventory is adjusted through use of a multiplier of 108/98, while the multiplier for the 1969 inventory is 108/106.

The monetary items (cash and claims to cash) in the 1968 balance sheet were expressed originally in terms of December 31, 1968, price levels rather than those existing at the time of their creation. Monetary items are always automatically expressed in terms of the current price level—a dollar of cash is always worth exactly one dollar of current purchasing power. And this explains why no adjustments are needed for the December 31, 1969, monetary items. But to compare with 1969 amounts, the 1968 amounts must be expressed in terms of 1969 price levels. Thus, the $20,000 of cash on hand on December 31, 1968, has a purchasing power equivalent to 21,600 December 31, 1969, dollars since prices rose 8 per cent (100 to 108) during the intervening year. The 1968 amounts for accounts payable and bonds payable are similarly adjusted. These adjustments are discussed further under the heading "Gains and Losses on Monetary Items." The amounts shown for retained earnings in each of the above balance sheets are simply the residuals required to balance the two statements. As will be shown later, they can be reconciled with income statement data.

Since all amounts are now expressed in common-dollar terms, the amounts may be validly compared and the differences adjudged real. And net income for the year, in terms of December 31, 1969, prices, can also be computed:

Retained earnings, December 31, 1969	$18,755
Dividends ($4,000 × 108/104)	4,154
	$22,909
Less: Retained earnings, December 31, 1968, in December 31, 1969 prices	15,800
Net income for the year	$ 7,109

It is assumed that dividends were declared and paid uniformly throughout the year. The multiplier to adjust money dividends into December 31, 1969, prices then is 108/104. The $7,109 represents income under an all-inclusive concept and, since its amount is positive and greater than dividends, capital measured in terms of purchasing power was maintained during the year. This income amount is now reconciled with that obtained under the transactions approach.

THE TRANSACTIONS APPROACH. The income statement for the year ended December 31, 1969, is presented below with all dollar amounts expressed in terms of December 31, 1969, price levels. It is assumed that sales, purchases, and other expenses and taxes were incurred and that prices increased uniformly throughout the year. As a result, these income statement items are adjusted by multiplying their historical amounts by a ratio consisting of the year-end index over the average index for the year, as indicated above. The adjustments for the beginning and ending inventories have already been discussed. The depreciation charge for the year must be doubled since it is originally expressed in terms of an index level of 54 while the current index is 108.

INCOME STATEMENT FOR YEAR ENDING DECEMBER 31, 1969
IN TERMS OF DECEMBER 31, 1969, PRICE LEVELS

Sales	(108/104)		$207,692
Cost of goods sold:			
Inventory, 12/31/68	(108/98)	$ 22,040	
Purchases	(108/104)	166,154	
		$188,194	
Inventory, 12/31/69	(108/106)	40,755	147,439
Gross margin			$ 60,253
Depreciation	(108/54)	$ 8,000	
Other expenses and taxes	(108/104)	47,769	55,769
Net income			$ 4,484

When all items are expressed in common-dollar terms, net income is $4,484 as compared to the mixed-dollar amount of $10,000 shown on the unadjusted income statement. And advocates of common-dollar accounting vigorously maintain that only after all items are expressed in the same unit of measure is the matching of expense and revenue properly carried out.

Typically, as illustrated in the above income statements, the major effects of changing price levels center around the depreciation or amortization charges on long-lived assets and on cost of goods sold. As a result practitioners sometimes suggest that these two items be adjusted and the other items, which are apt to be immaterial, be ignored since their adjustment creates only needless complexity.[25] Such a procedure is, of course, incomplete and may produce biased information by ignoring substantial gains and losses from holding monetary items. *Accounting Research Study No. 6* rightfully rejects this approach.[26]

[25] See "Comments of Robert C. Tyson," *Accounting Research Study No. 6, op. cit.,* pp. 252–253.
[26] *Ibid.,* pp. xi–xii.

GAINS AND LOSSES ON MONETARY ITEMS. The loss of purchasing power sustained when cash (or other claims to a fixed sum of money) is held during a period of rising prices is easily demonstrated. Assume that a man held $1,000 of cash during a year in which prices rose 50 per cent. Although he still has his $1,000 at the end of the year, he has suffered a loss of $500 (in year-end dollars) since 1,500 year-end dollars are needed to give him the same command over goods and services that he possessed at the beginning of the year. He has lost one-third of his purchasing power ($500/ $1,500). The loss can also be expressed in terms of beginning-of-the-year dollars as $333. He has at the end of the year $1,000, which has purchasing power equivalent to $667 in beginning-of-the-year dollars ($1,000 × 100/150).

That a gain accrues to a debtor in an inflationary period is based on the assumption that money incomes will increase as price levels rise, with the result that the actual economic sacrifice required to pay a fixed obligation decreases. Thus, a debtor owing $600 during a year in which prices rise 40 per cent experiences a gain of $240 in year-end dollars. The original debt has a year-end purchasing power equivalent of $840 ($600 × 140/100), but since it can be satisfied through payment of $600, a gain accrues.

The company, in the extended illustration above, experienced a gain of $3,200 from being indebted on bonds payable throughout the year. It also suffered a $575 loss on monetary working capital (cash minus accounts payable) during the same period. The computation of this gain or loss is somewhat more complex since the items involved change continuously throughout the year. Here the computation is simplified by assuming that all changes occurred uniformly throughout the year and can therefore be deemed to occur at the average of the price index for the year. And because of the uniform flow assumption, only the net monetary working capital need be adjusted, as follows:

Monetary working capital at December 31, 1968, expressed in December 31, 1969, prices ($20,000–$8,000) × (108/100)	$12,960
Decrease ($12,000–$2,000) during the year adjusted to year-end dollars ($10,000 × 108/104)	10,385
Monetary working capital balance needed at year-end if no gain or loss is involved	$ 2,575
Actual monetary working capital	2,000
Loss on holding monetary working capital during the year	$ 575

The following reconciliation can now be made:

Net income, per adjusted income statement	$ 4,484
Gain on holding long-term debt	3,200
Loss on holding monetary working capital	(575)
Net income, per adjusted balance-sheet approach	$ 7,109

THE REALIZATION OF MONETARY GAINS.   Beginning with Sweeney, accountants have attempted to apply their realization concept to gains resulting from holding monetary items.[27] Realization was deemed to occur when a transaction caused the item to be paid, used, or to leave the firm. Thus, a gain from being indebted on long-term bonds payable would not be considered realized until the bonds were redeemed.

Others have taken the position that gains and losses on monetary working capital items can, as a practical matter, be considered realized as they occur because of their rapid turnover. But gains on long-term debt should be considered realized only when the debt is paid.[28] Both of these approaches would presumably call for the inclusion of an unrealized gain account in the balance sheet and the attendant difficulty of classifying it properly as a liability or stockholders' equity item.

Under yet another interpretation the gain from being indebted on long-term debt (or all debt) during an inflationary period is not considered a gain at all but a form of cost savings and is deducted from the assets acquired with the debt.[29] This approach suffers from conceptual deficiencies in addition to the practical problem of having to deal with an asset without knowing its cost until it is paid for, which might be some time later. The cost of the asset acquired is considered to be the purchasing power surrendered to obtain it rather than its historical cost adjusted for price level changes. Assume, for example, that a tract of land is acquired for the $100,000 proceeds of a bond issue. Under this approach, the land will always be carried at $100,000 as long as the debt is outstanding, regardless of what happens to the price level. If prices double, the land will be restated at $200,000 and then the $100,000 gain on the debt deducted. If the

---

[27] Henry W. Sweeney, *Stabilized Accounting* (New York: Harper & Bros., 1936), pp. 21–23.

[28] Perry Mason, *Price-Level Changes and Financial Statements — Basic Concepts and Methods* (American Accounting Association, 1956), fn., pp. 23–24.

[29] *Accounting Research Study No. 6, op. cit.*, pp. 153–165 and 251.

price level rises five-fold and the debt is paid off when it has doubled, the land would be carried at $400,000. Yet the very purpose of introducing price level adjustments is to restate conventional measurements in common terms, *not to change basic concepts.*

The approach is also conceptually deficient because it attempts to relate two unrelated items. Assume that the land was acquired in 1959 when the price level stood at 100, that by 1969 prices had doubled, and that the bonds were still outstanding. Assume further that comparative balance sheets are to be prepared, expressed in 1959 dollars. The land would be shown at $100,000 for both dates. But the bonds would be shown at $100,000 in the 1959 statement and at $50,000 in the 1969 statement. The $100,000 obligation owed in 1969 has a purchasing power of $50,000 in 1959 dollars, and a gain of $50,000 in 1959 dollars has resulted. The gain could be translated into 1969 dollars simply by multiplying by 200/100; but whether expressed in 1959 or 1969 dollars, it is still equal to 50 per cent of the original purchasing power invested. Thus, the gain can be seen to exist independently of the dollar measurement attached to the land.[30]

Accounting Research Study No. 6 includes the purchasing power gains on debt in arriving at a final income statement amount labeled "net profit and net inflation gain (loss)." [31] *A Statement of Basic Accounting Theory* includes these gains and losses in arriving at an amount called "net income." [32] It would seem proper to hold that, if these gains and losses are brought to light by measurements considered sufficiently verifiable to warrant their inclusion in balance sheets, they are sufficiently verifiable to be included in the income statement.

INTERPRETATION OF ADJUSTED DATA.   As has been noted, price level adjusted data are especially useful in highlighting real interperiod changes. They can also have a substantial effect upon some of the heavily relied upon analytical ratios. For example, the adjusted and the unadjusted rates of return upon average stockholders' equity in the above illustration are 3.3 per cent and 9.3 per cent. Elimination of the largely uncontrollable effects of price level changes brought about a substantial lowering of this ratio. In view of the long-run upward trend of prices in our economy, it seems likely that

[30] *Ibid.,* p. 42.
[31] *Ibid.,* p. 128
[32] *Op. cit.,* pp. 85, 95.

the older the assets employed the higher will be the unadjusted rate of return compared to its adjusted counterpart.[33]

AN UNRESOLVED ISSUE.   A still unresolved question is what index number to use in measuring the purchasing-power equivalents of the capital to be maintained. Because an individual can choose between business investment and consumers' goods, it is maintained that general purchasing power — command over all goods and services — is the appropriate criterion. But funds once invested in a business entity are reinvested by that entity, not by the investor, so the investor has no continuing choice.

It is sometimes urged that, since all investments in producers' goods are to enhance consumption, capital should be measured in terms of its command over consumers' goods and services. But investors generally consume the income from capital, not the capital itself, which is recouped and reinvested by the entity in producers' goods.

If purchasing power is to be measured in terms of command over producers' goods, should the index employed be a measure of the price movements of all producers' goods, of the producers' goods usually acquired by firms in the industry, or of the producers' goods usually acquired by the specific firm? Since firms do diversify, the first approach is probably preferable. And the use of a single producers' goods index would enhance interfirm comparability of data.[34]

But should an index based solely on producers' goods be used? Probably not. Assume, for example, that $100,000 is invested in an entity which purchases a tract of land for $100,000, holds it a number of years, and then sells it for $200,000. Assume further that during this period an index of general purchasing power rose 60 per cent, while an index of land values doubled. Income is either $40,000 or zero depending upon which price level index is used to adjust the purchase price.

To hold that income is zero seems quite inconsistent with the fact that the entity has increased its ability to command goods and services by $40,000. For this reason, an index of general purchasing power seems preferable and is supported in *Accounting Research Study No. 6*.[35] This would be especially true in order to maintain

---

[33] See the results of actual case studies reported in *Accounting Research Study No. 6, op. cit.*, Appendix E.

[34] For a full discussion of this issue, see Hendriksen, *op. cit.*, pp. 177–182.

[35] *Op. cit.*, p. xi.

equity between taxpayers if price level adjusted data are ever accepted for tax purposes.

Current Cost

The notion that measurements of income and other financial data may possess greater utility when expressed in current terms has long been supported by accountants, principally academicians, especially in recent years.[36] The current cost of an asset is usually the price that would have to be paid currently to replace it, and this price may differ substantially from the asset's historical cost adjusted by either an index of general or specific prices. Practitioners generally reject the concept because it cannot be implemented in objective terms,[37] although there are exceptions.[38]

The advocacy of current cost is usually based upon one or more of the following reasons: (1) Managements are motivated by their expectations about the prices of specific goods and not by the average prices reflected in general price level indices. (2) A proper appraisal of managerial effectiveness requires the separation of planned income from purely windfall or fortuitous gains — that is, operating income must be distinguished from holding gains and losses. (3) The utility of information for predictive purposes is greatly enhanced when operating income is expressed as the excess of revenues over the current cost of the assets consumed in producing them. (4) Data expressed in current cost terms are more readily comparable between entities.

THE AAA APPROACH.   As defined by the various committees of the American Accounting Association, current cost is the cost of replacing the specific asset consumed in the generation of revenues. If,

[36] Committee on Accounting Concepts and Standards, *Accounting and Reporting Standards for Corporate Financial Statements: 1957 Revision* (American Accounting Association, 1957), p. 6, and the *Supplementary Statements No. 1 and No. 2* thereto in *The Accounting Review,* (July 1964), pp. 693–714; *A Statement of Basic Accounting Theory, op. cit.;* Edwards and Bell, *op. cit.* For early support, see W. A. Paton, "The Significance and Treatment of Appreciation in the Accounts," *Twentieth Annual Report of the Michigan Academy of Sciences, 1918,* as reprinted in *Paton on Accounting,* Herbert F. Taggart, ed. (Ann Arbor: The University of Michigan Bureau of Business Research, 1964), pp. 21–35. Also see references cited in Edwards and Bell, *op. cit.,* pp. 26–27 fn.

[37] See "Comments of Russell H. Morrison," in *A Statement of Basic Accounting Theory, op. cit.,* pp. 97–98.

[38] See Howard Ross, *The Elusive Art of Accounting* (New York: The Ronald Press Company, 1966).

because of technological advances, the specific asset is no longer available, the cost of acquiring services equivalent to those provided by the asset consumed is substituted.

To illustrate the Association's approach, assume that a company acquired two units of a product at $50 each when a general price index stood at 100. One of the units is sold for $100 at year-end when the price index stands at 110 and when the cost of replacing the unit sold is $57. A properly drawn income statement would show sales of $100 less $57 cost of goods sold, leaving a gross margin of $43. A holding gain on inventory of $4, two units at $2 each, would also be reported. The $2 is the excess of replacement cost over the historical cost of the unit, adjusted for general price level change ($50 × 110/100). The $5 increase in the recorded cost of each unit would be a restatement of the capital invested, not an element of income.

THE EDWARDS AND BELL APPROACH.   This is quite similar to the AAA approach, except for the recommendation that the current cost of the actual assets employed or consumed, not the current cost of equivalent assets, be deducted from revenues in arriving at current operating profit.[39] Edwards and Bell assert that operating income determined in this manner will reveal, through interfirm comparisons, the truly efficient productive processes. Their model also permits distinguishing between realized and unrealized holding gains, if desired. Under one interpretation of realization, only $2 of the $4 of holding gains in the above example would be called realized. That relating to the unit not sold would be called a realizable gain.

THE PHYSICAL CAPACITY APPROACH.   A third current cost approach embraces the notion that income does not emerge until the cost of replacing the capital consumed in operations has been deducted from revenues. Here emphasis is upon capital maintenance in the sense of the physical capacity to produce.[40] The results obtained from following this approach are essentially similar to those obtained when the purchasing power of capital is measured with an index based upon the prices paid by a specific firm for producers' goods. If applied in the above example, the entire $14 (two units

[39] Edwards and Bell, op. cit., p. 186.

[40] Jean St. G. Kerr, "Three Concepts of Business Income," The Australian Accountant, Vol. 26 (April 1956), p. 141. Reprinted in An Income Approach to Accounting Theory, Sidney Davidson, David Green, Jr., Charles T. Horngren, and George H. Sorter, eds. (Englewood Cliffs, N. J.: Prentice-Hall, Inc., 1964), p. 44.

at $7) would be carried to stockholders' equity as a capital adjustment rather than treated partially as a holding gain and partially as capital.

Where price level adjustments have been introduced into financial statements, this third approach has typically been employed.[41] But the theoretical propriety and equity of this approach is subject to question, for the reasons presented when discussing whether an index of producers' goods should be employed. It should be noted that LIFO embraces this concept of income. Typically, the increase in the replacement cost of the goods on hand is not recognized. But some recommend that the increase in value be recognized and credited to an account treated as an element of capital.[42]

Income Inclusions and Exclusions

The increased emphasis upon income and especially the heavy reliance upon an earnings per share amount as a single index of profitability and progress have raised the issue of what exactly should be included in net income for the year. Inclusion or exclusion from net income of two major items is controversial: (1) unusual, nonrecurring, and perhaps unexpected items not directly related to ordinary operations, and (2) adjustments or revisions of prior period estimates — a natural result of the uncertainty surrounding many of the accountant's assignments of expense and revenue to given periods.

THE ALL-INCLUSIVE CONCEPT. Under this concept, all items affecting total owners' equity, except capital transactions and dividends, are to be included in arriving at net income for the year they are recognized. The income account is the only door to retained earnings, and the total net income of the entity is the sum of all of its previous annual net incomes. The successive income statements form a complete historical narrative of the results of operations, and only when prepared in this way are they a fair report on such operations, or so some maintain.

Supporters also claim that a number of specific advantages

[41] See Appendix D of *Accounting Research Study No. 6, op. cit.* Also see A. Goudeket, "An Application of Replacement Value Theory," *The Journal of Accountancy*, Vol. 110 (July 1960), p. 38, and comments by Willard Graham in "Letters," *The Journal of Accountancy*, Vol. 110 (August 1960), pp. 28–31.

[42] H. T. McAnly, "The Case for Lifo: It Realistically States Income and Is Applicable in Any Industry," *The Journal of Accountancy*, Vol. 95 (June 1953), p. 698.

follow from including all items of income or loss in arriving at net income:

1. Such full disclosure tends to prevent persons not knowledgeable of accounting practices from overlooking items which may affect appraisal of an entity. At the same time, informed persons can recast the data in any manner they believe useful.
2. The opportunities to manipulate income—for example, by writing depreciable assets off to retained earnings to reduce future depreciation charges are reduced.
3. A more objective income amount is reported—one free from subjective interpretations of what is operating or nonoperating, extraordinary or ordinary, or recurring or nonrecurring. As a result the income statement is easier to prepare.
4. There is avoidance of income overstatement resulting from the fact that unfavorable extraordinary items tend to bulk larger than favorable ones.
5. Bias in income reporting is eliminated. It has been documented that favorable extraordinary items tend to be reported in the income statement while unfavorable ones are reported in the retained earnings statement.[43]

THE CURRENT OPERATING PERFORMANCE CONCEPT. Under this concept, only the results of normal, regular, recurring operations are included in current income. The income effects of extraordinary transactions and prior period adjustments are carried to retained earnings.

Advocates of this concept stress the use of income measurements in appraising managerial efficiency and in predicting future incomes. To be useful for these purposes, current income should include only the results of controllable activities resulting from current decisions. When so computed, current income can be compared with prior incomes and valid conclusions can be drawn about trends. Current income can readily be compared with similarly computed incomes of other entities, and it serves as a valid basis for prediction since it is based upon operations expected to recur.

But this concept involves several questionable assumptions, and objectives may be at least partially conflicting. The income for a period, for example, can never solely reflect current decisions simply because long-lived assets acquired years earlier are often

[43] Leopold A. Bernstein, "The Concept of Materiality," *The Accounting Review*, Vol. 42 (January 1967), p. 87.

involved. And managerial efficiency may be involved in generating nonoperating income. Consequently, a proper appraisal of efficiency may involve comparing against some standard all incomes produced. Yet in the absence of such standards (or knowledge of standards), probably the best course is to compare results of current operations against similar data for other periods or firms. But under this procedure, the income effects of prior period adjustments are likely to be excluded entirely in appraising efficiency unless historical summaries of revised incomes are used.

Using income determined under this concept to predict implicitly assumes that income from operations is recurring and that nonoperating income is not. Clearly, nonoperating income may be recurring and, if so, should be included in income measurements used for prediction.

The advocates of this concept also argue that many users of income statements prepared under an all-inclusive concept are not qualified to eliminate the effects of extraordinary items or prior period adjustments to get the income amount they seek. This task should, therefore, be completed by someone qualified — the accountant. They also argue that including a correction of a prior year's income in a current year's income misstates the incomes of both years. Trend analyses may, as a result, be misleading.

Treating extraordinary items and prior period adjustments as direct adjustments of retained earnings is also asserted to be the simplest, least confusing manner of handling such items. For example, an annual report may, under the all-inclusive concept, contain an income statement for 1969 showing an additional assessment of income taxes for 1965 as an item used in arriving at net income. If, as is frequently the case, an historical summary of earnings is presented, the tax assessment may be shown there as a 1965 expense. Thus, the same annual report contains two different income amounts for 1969. This possible source of confusion would be eliminated under the current operating performance concept.

APB OPINION NO. 9.   As noted in Chapter 2, the American Accounting Association has in the past strongly supported, and the Securities Exchange Commission has sought to move toward, requiring use of the all-inclusive approach to income reporting. On the surface the American Institute has been on middle ground; Chapter 8 of *Accounting Research Bulletin No. 43* at first seems to direct that all items having an income effect recognized during a period be included in arriving at net income for the period. But immediately an exception is granted for items which in the aggregate are "materially significant in relation to a company's net income" and clearly not identifiable with or resulting from the typical operations of the period.[44] As a consequence, practice varies widely.[45]

In an attempt to narrow practice in this area, the Accounting Principles Board stated in *Opinion No. 9* "that net income should reflect all items of profit and loss recognized during the period with the sole exception of . . . prior period adjustments . . . ."[46] As defined by the Board, prior period adjustments which should be excluded from current net income are

those material adjustments which (a) can be specifically identified with and directly related to the business activities of particular prior periods, and (b) are not attributable to economic events occurring subsequent to the date of the financial statements for the prior period, and (c) depend primarily on determinations by persons other than management, and (d) were not susceptible of reasonable estimation prior to such determination.[47]

In the opinion of the Board, prior period adjustments will be rare. In most instances, they will relate to a period for which the auditor's opinion was qualified because of uncertainty surrounding the item in question. They will probably arise from items such as income tax settlements, contract renegotiations, and litigation. Ruled out from consideration as prior period adjustments are adjustments resulting from changes in the estimated lives of depreciable assets, immaterial adjustments in the estimates of liabilities, and the differences between amounts realized from and recorded amounts for certain assets if intervening economic events affected the amounts realized. But however practical it may be to correct errors in depreciation by spreading remaining depreciable amounts over remaining lives, it is still an espousal of a theory that two wrongs make a right. And in some circumstances a currently recognized loss on an asset might be definitely related to a prior period.[48] A loss,

[44] Paragraph 11.

[45] Bernstein, *op. cit.*, pp. 86–87.

[46] Accounting Principles Board, "Reporting the Results of Operations," *Opinion No. 9*, December 1966 (New York: American Institute of Certified Public Accountants, 1967), para. 17.

[47] *Ibid.*, para. 23.

[48] See qualified assent of George Catlett, *ibid.*, para. 52.

first discovered in the current period, may actually have existed and occurred in a prior period.

In an affort to abstract the best of the all-inclusive and current operating performance concepts, *Opinion No. 9* also recommends that extraordinary items be reported (net of income taxes) as additions to or deductions from "income before extraordinary items" in arriving at "net income."[49] Extraordinary items are those not related to customary business activities and not expected to recur frequently.

How well the Board's approach will work remains to be seen. Problems are likely to arise in distinguishing between extraordinary and ordinary items and between extraordinary items and prior period adjustments. And the Opinion continues the unsatisfactory standard by stating that the materiality of an item is determined through an exercise of judgment.[50]

SUMMARY

Although noting their conceptual value as models, the accountant believes that psychic income and economic income are unimplementable concepts because they cannot be verifiably measured. Although the accountant measures capital in terms of money investment rather than in terms of well being or real wealth, he does accept the economist's notion that income does not exist until capital has been maintained. And the accountant articulates his transactions (income statement) approach to income measurement with the balance sheet approach as implied in the economist's view of income as a change in wealth.

A strong probability exists that, under increased inflation, supplemental financial statements will be regularly presented to measure income and capital maintenance in terms of purchasing power. As a matter of theory and equity, such purchasing power is best measured through an index of general, rather than specific, prices.

Although strongly supported in the literature, the use of replacement cost as a basis of asset valuation and in income determination has received little direct support from practitioners.

Opinion No. 9 of the Accounting Principles Board favors the all-inclusive concept over the current operating performance concept of income reporting.

[49] *Ibid.*, para. 20.
[50] *Ibid.*, para. 21.

QUESTIONS

1. In what respects have the uses for measurements of income changed in our society over the last 30 to 40 years?

2. Does the attempt to measure income represent a trade-off between reality and objectivity? Explain.

3. What are some of the noneconomic components of psychic income?

4. Define, then criticize or defend, the economic concept of income.

5. Ideally, there is only one measure of the income for a given entity for a specified period of time. Discuss.

6. Because the accountant and the economist both deal with measurements of economic resources, their concepts of income should be the same. Discuss.

7. (a) What are the economist's major criticisms of the accounting concept of income? (b) Evaluate each criticism.

8. What are the advantages and disadvantages of determining income via the transactions approach?

9. Cite several examples of practices which will support the contention that the accountant does not have a single concept of income.

10. Give several examples of currently accepted accounting practices which yield an income amount consistent with capital maintenance measured in terms of replacement cost.

11. (a) Why might expected and actual subjective income differ? (b) What additional problems must be resolved if they do differ?

12. "It has been established, at least in theory, that many users of financial statements need projections of cash flow and little else in order to make intelligent decisions." Explain how these individuals use cash flows to make decisions.

13. Does the fact that replacement of an asset is not anticipated represent a barrier to application of an income concept based on capital maintenance measured in terms of replacement cost? Explain.

14. (a) How can it be argued that any measure of income based on asset measurements in terms of market values is incomplete? (b) Or is of little value to a stockholder?

15. (a) Assume that the historical cost of a tract of land of $100,000 is adjusted through use of an index of general prices, with the result that the land is restated at $180,000. What is the proper description of this $180,000? (b) Can it properly be referred to as current cost or value? Why?

16. How might an economist criticize the income reported on an income

statement in which all data have been adjusted for general price level change?

17. Explain carefully how a gain allegedly accrues to a net debtor in a period of inflation.

18. Given the following data, compute the gain or loss from holding monetary working capital during that year:

Cash and accounts receivable, 12/31/68	$75,000
Cash and accounts receivable, 12/31/69	80,000
Current liabilities, 12/31/68	25,000
Current liabilities, 12/31/69	28,000

A given price index rose from 100 to 104 during the year.

19. Any inflation gain accruing on bonds outstanding should be treated as a cost savings and deducted from the cost of the assets acquired with the proceeds of the bonds issue. Discuss.

20. When attempting to measure periodic income, what is the conceptual deficiency in using a producers' goods index to determine whether capital has been maintained?

21. Assume that an asset was acquired at a cost of $40 when a general price index stood at 100. The asset was sold later for $50 when this index stood at 110 and when the asset's replacement cost was $45. What are the net income, holding gain, and the capital adjustment under each of the following?
(a) The psychic income concept.
(b) The conventional transactions approach to income measurement.
(c) The current cost approach to income measurement:
    (1) the AAA method.
    (2) the physical capacity method.
What would be the difficulties in attempting to apply the AAA method to inventories in an actual company?

22. Which of the alternative approaches to income reporting—all-inclusive or current operating performance—provides the better basis for predicting future net income? Why?

23. (a) How has the Accounting Principles Board's *Opinion No. 9* attempted to resolve the all-inclusive versus current operating performance income reporting controversy? (b) What problems remain unresolved?

24. In practice, what major limitation or disadvantage has been found to exist in attempting to report income under the current operating performance concept? Explain.

5

REVENUES
AND
EXPENSES

Income determination is a central activity in modern accounting practice. This fact, together with the transactions approach to income determination, tends to explain why attention to the nature, measurement, and time of recognition of revenues and expenses pervades most of what is done in accounting today. In fact, it can be argued that no real comprehension of current financial accounting theory and practice is obtainable until it is fully recognized that the balance sheet contains residuals in the income determining process.[1] What is reported in the balance sheet is largely determined by the principles and practices employed to present an income statement. For example, tax allocation is usually justified on the grounds that it is necessary in order to reflect income properly rather than that an asset or liability actually exists. This contention will be further supported by the presentation and discussion in this chapter of current practice and theory of revenue and expense recognition.

REVENUE RECOGNITION

The primary areas of concern in the accounting for revenues — its nature, measurement, and time of recognition — are discussed below. Considerable attention is centered on the time of recognition, as this has proven to be of greatest interest in practice. This will be followed by a presentation and discussion of currently accepted practices of revenue recognition.

[1] This notion that the balance sheet contains residuals or remainders was first expressed by an Austrian writer in the late 1800s. See A. C. Littleton, *Accounting Evolution to 1900* (New York: American Institute Publishing Co., Inc., 1933), pp. 178–181.

Revenue Defined

Revenue, like income, is a flow concept and could be defined in nonmonetary terms as the productive accomplishment or net product—goods and services—of an entity.[2] But, since accounting deals in money measurements, revenue is defined as the monetary expression of the goods created or the services rendered.[3] Note that there is no requirement for the goods to have been delivered (as stated in the American Accounting Association's 1957 Statement).[4] Such a requirement would narrow the definition too much since revenues can be recognized before goods are delivered. And, for the same reason, defining revenues as resulting from the sale of goods is unduly narrow.[5]

Revenue has also been defined as an increase in net assets or as an inflow of assets resulting from the production or delivery of goods or the rendering of services.[6] But, as Hendriksen points out, these definitions confuse the measurement of revenue with the revenue process.[7]

The term "productive accomplishment" includes what are often described as the nonoperating activities of an entity.[8] The results of such activities—interest, dividends, rent—are properly included in the definition of revenue.

Revenue has been defined to exclude gains arising from the sale, exchange, or conversion of assets other than stock in trade (inventory).[9] Such gains are excluded primarily because they do not

[2] W. A. Paton and A. C. Littleton, *An Introduction to Corporate Accounting Standards* (American Accounting Association, 1940), pp. 46–47.

[3] Robert T. Sprouse and Maurice Moonitz, "A Tentative Set of Broad Accounting Principles for Business Enterprises," *Accounting Research Study No. 3* (New York: American Institute of Certified Public Accountants, 1961), p. 46.

[4] Committee on Accounting Concepts and Standards, *Accounting and Reporting Standards for Corporate Financial Statements and Preceding Statements and Supplements* (American Accounting Association, 1957), p. 5.

[5] This definition is from *Accounting Terminology Bulletin No. 2* and is cited and supported in Paul Grady, "Inventory of Generally Accepted Accounting Principles for Business Enterprises," *Accounting Research Study No. 7*, (New York: American Institute of Certified Public Accountants, 1965), pp. 74–75.

[6] See Sprouse and Moonitz, *op. cit.*, p. 46. Also see the 1948 Statement of the Committee on Accounting Concepts and Standards, *op. cit.*, p. 15.

[7] Eldon S. Hendriksen, *Accounting Theory* (Homewood, Ill.: Richard D. Irwin, Inc., 1965), p. 129.

[8] Paton and Littleton, *op. cit.*, pp. 47–48.

[9] *Ibid.*, p. 47. See also, Sprouse and Moonitz, *op. cit.*, p. 46, and *Accounting and Reporting Standards for Corporate Financial Statements, op. cit.*, p. 15.

relate to the usual productive activity of the entity and are often nonrecurring. Furthermore, only the gain itself is usually recorded since the selling price or gross amount received is not considered an indicator of entity accomplishment as are the other elements included in revenue. On the other hand, such gains are, according to APB *Opinion No. 9,* extraordinary items which are be shown net of applicable income taxes in arriving at net income and are, therefore, implicitly elements of revenue.[10] *A Statement of Basic Accounting Theory* also implies that such gains are elements of revenue.[11] But to achieve consistent and clear usage, revenue in this text implies a gross concept.

Revenue Measurement

The revenue of an entity is best measured by the immediate exchange value of its goods and services. In current practice, revenue is typically recorded at the price established in the agreement reached with the customer. But this price measures the exchange value and the revenue involved only when cash is received immediately. And even then an occasional adjustment may be required for expected returns and allowances.

If a claim to cash rather than cash is received, the present value of the claim must be determined either through reference to money markets or by a discounting process. A sale in which a $1,000 non-interest-bearing note, due in one year, is received does not, for example, yield $1,000 of revenue if the present worth of the note is only $940. Revenue from the sale of product is only $940 and the additional $60 ultimately collected is a measure of the revenue generated by the resource-loaning activities of the entity.

In actual practice, the discounting of promises to pay future sums is usually ignored because (1) questions arise about what interest rate to employ; (2) since short-term promises are involved, the amounts are likely to be immaterial; (3) even if the implicit interest is material, the effect on periodic income is apt to be immaterial since the discounting process involves largely a reclassifi-

---

[10] Accounting Principles Board, "Reporting the Results of Operations," *Opinion No. 9* (New York: American Institute of Certified Public Accountants, December 1966), pp. 114, 133ff.

[11] Committee to Prepare a Statement of Basic Accounting Theory, *A Statement of Basic Accounting Theory* (Evanston, Ill.: American Accounting Association, 1966), p. 85.

cation of revenues into product sales and interest revenue, which may not be significant information.[12]

Revenue is often measured by valuing the asset received, and the value of an asset is its future expected net receipts appropriately discounted for interest and probability factors.[13] Since cash discounts, returns, and other allowances reduce the amount of cash inflow expected, they reduce the value of the asset. And it follows that these items also reduce the amount of revenue involved and should be accounted for as revenue reductions.

Similarly, it can be argued that estimated uncollectible amounts of accounts receivable arising from sales of products and services are reductions in recorded revenues, not expenses. A sale on account of $100, which has a most probable value of $97, yields $97 of revenue, not $100 of revenue and $3 of expense. And since a primary reason for granting cash discounts is to reduce uncollectible accounts, another reason exists for treating discounts as revenue reductions rather than expenses. Hendriksen further argues that if cash discount rates are established rationally, the seller would be indifferent about whether he collected the net amount on sales or a larger gross amount reduced by expected uncollectible amounts.[14]

When an entity functions merely as a collecting agency, as in the case of freight costs advanced or sales taxes levied, the services provided are not those of the entity. Such amounts should not be included in its revenue.[15]

The Time of Revenue Recognition

Accountants have long subscribed to the general guides that revenue should be recorded only after the activities undertaken to create it have been substantially completed and it can be verifiably measured.[16] Briefly, these may be referred to as the earning and realization of revenue.

---

[12] For a further discussion of this point and an illustration of the procedures involved, see W. A. Paton and W. A. Paton, Jr., *Asset Accounting* (New York: The Macmillan Company, 1952), pp. 19–20.

[13] *Accounting and Reporting Standards for Corporate Financial Statements, op. cit.*, p. 4.

[14] Hendriksen, *op. cit.*, p. 131.

[15] Sprouse and Moonitz, *op. cit.*, p. 46.

[16] E. A. Heilman, "Realized Revenue," *The Accounting Review*, Vol. 4 (June 1929), pp. 80–87.

THE EARNING PROCESS. Accountants accept the general notion that virtually all of the activities of an entity are undertaken to produce revenue even though it is conventionally recognized at the time of the sale of the product created. As a result, revenue is assumed to be earned through time as the various factors of production are brought together to create a product or render a service.[17]

In certain situations, such as the lending of money at interest, revenue may readily be conceived of as being earned moment by moment through time as the debtor has possession of the funds advanced by the creditor. Similarly, the notion can be accepted that exchange value is being created as a product moves along an assembly line in a large and complex business entity to emerge physically completed at the end of the line. This is especially so if a brisk demand exists for the product. But if the demand has been created by advertising which altered the tastes and desires of individuals, the advertising activity is also revenue producing. Thus, in the broad sense, all business activity is revenue producing.

But the accountant faces a difficult task in attempting to record the revenue produced by the various activities of an entity. Satisfactory measures of revenue may be available where a product is produced and sold by one division of an entity to another which uses the part to assemble a product to be sold to outsiders. But since market values do not exist for, say, an automobile before and after a door is installed, most attempts to assign revenue to individual activities will involve arbitrary allocations of the revenue produced jointly by these activities. Where revenues are recognized as production progresses, unless evidence exists to the contrary, the assumption is made that all costs incurred produce equal amounts of revenue. Since it is unlikely that an entity is equally efficient in performing all of its activities, the assumption is conceptually unsatisfactory.[18]

In smaller, single-division, or single-plant entities, the accountant typically refuses to recognize revenue until substantially all of the activity required to produce it has been completed. Revenue is often recognized in multidivision or multicorporation entities when products are transferred between divisions or entities. But the

[17] Paton and Littleton, *op. cit.*, p. 48. See also George O. May, *Financial Accounting* (New York: The Macmillan Company, 1943), pp. 30–31.

[18] Concepts and Standards Research Study Committee, "The Realization Concept," *The Accounting Review*, Vol. 40 (April 1965), pp. 316–317.

income related to such revenues is eliminated in the preparation of the consolidated financial statements if the product has not been sold to outsiders.

REALIZATION.   Realization is undoubtedly one of the most important principles in accounting.[19] Unfortunately, there is no agreement about its precise meaning and the extent to which it is to be applied. Sprouse and Moonitz reject the term and the notion itself because (1) it lacks analytical precision, (2) it conflicts, by emphasizing the act of sale, with the postulated continuity of business activity, and (3) its application may assign revenues to the wrong period, that is, to the period of sale rather than the period of earning.[20]

Realization is broadly defined and not related directly to revenue recognition in the American Accounting Association's 1957 Statement. Here realization is held to mean "that a change in an asset or a liability has become sufficiently definite and objective to warrant recognition in the accounts."[21] All such changes are to be analyzed for their source and, if related to the product of the entity, recognized as revenue.

As previously noted, the U. S. Supreme Court has held that growths in the value of assets constitute realized income only when severed from capital and placed in disposable or distributable form.[22] And these notions underlie the practitioner's view that realization occurs when a sale — loosely defined as a market transaction — has occurred and when liquid (cash or near-cash) assets have been received. Yet a more accurate depiction of economic activity would probably result if emphasis were placed upon

---

[19] Reed K. Storey, "Revenue Realization, Going Concern and Measurement of Income," *The Accounting Review,* Vol. 34 (April 1959), p. 238. For other discussions of realization, see Charles T. Horngren, "How Should We Interpret the Realization Concept?" *The Accounting Review,* Vol. 40 (April 1965), pp. 323–333; Sidney Davidson, "The Realization Concept," in *Modern Accounting Theory,* Morton Backer, ed. (Englewood Cliffs, N.J.: Prentice-Hall, Inc., 1966), pp. 99–116; Floyd W. Windal, "The Accounting Concept of Realization," *The Accounting Review,* Vol. 36 (April 1961), pp. 249–258, and "Legal Background for the Accounting Concept of Realization," *The Accounting Review,* Vol. 38 (January 1963), pp. 29–36; Harold E. Arnett, "Recognition as a Function of Measurement in the Realization Concept," *The Accounting Review,* Vol. 38 (October 1963), pp. 733–741.

[20] *Op. cit.,* pp. 14–17.

[21] *Accounting and Reporting Standards for Corporate Financial Statements, op. cit.,* p. 3. See also William J. Vatter, "Another Look at the 1957 Statement," *The Accounting Review,* Vol. 37 (October 1962), and George J. Staubus, "Comments on the 1957 Revision," *The Accounting Review,* Vol. 33 (January 1958), p. 21.

[22] *Eisner v. Macomber,* 25 U.S. 188, 195 (1920).

measurable rather than liquid assets.[23] Note also that the receipt of a liquid asset is not required to support the recognition of revenue where a concurrent market transaction is not involved, such as in the accumulation of discount on bond investments.

Holding that realization involves participation in a market transaction rules out the recording of a market value by all except the parties to the transaction establishing it. In this way, increases in the value of assets held — holding gains — even where readily verifiable are considered unrealized. Yet it can be argued that the bulk of the revenue recognized in practice today is supported by a market transaction or a logical extension of such a transaction. This is true even, for example, of the accrual of interest and the recognition of revenue on a percentage-of-completion basis on long-term contracts. But an exception still exists for revenue recognized upon the completion of production in certain industries as discussed below.

From the practitioner's viewpoint, then, realization is not a universal principle; it is a general guide, requiring certain exceptions. For example, the market prices of certain agricultural and mineral products may be considered sufficiently definite and objective to serve as a basis for revenue recognition. The expected selling prices for heterogeneous, nonstaple goods may not be. But the practitioner's constant refusal to recognize the definite and objective increase in the value of marketable securities as revenue seems justifiable only if the term "definite" is understood to mean permanent.[24]

In recent definitions of realization, the distinction between the earning of revenue and its realization is obliterated. Here realization consists of three tests: (1) verifiable evidence of a value increase, (2) a market transaction between the accounting unit and an outsider, and (3) the delivery of goods or the rendering of services.[25] Thus, the cash advance which previously could be called unearned revenue is now to be called unrealized revenue. It is questionable whether this fusion of the earnings test into the realization test will lead to better understanding and clarity in communication.

But the position advocated may attract some support from users of financial information. Its advocates urge recognition of value

---

[23] Concepts and Standards Research Study Committee, *op. cit.*, p. 315.

[24] Windal, "Legal Background for the Accounting Concept of Realization," *op. cit.*, p. 36.

[25] Concepts and Standards Research Study Committee, *op. cit.*, pp. 315–317; Davidson, *op. cit.*, pp. 102–108; Horngren, *op. cit.*, p. 325.

changes based on verifiable evidence, with such changes carried as unrealized gains until realized via a market transaction. In this way additional information users consider valuable may be provided.[26]

THE CRITICAL EVENT. Because revenue is the product of joint activities, when should revenue be considered earned? A proposed solution calls for viewing revenue as earned when the event or activity most critical or crucial to its production has been completed.[27]

The concept of the crucial event can be illustrated with a cash sale of a three-year magazine subscription. Conventionally, the revenue is allocated uniformly to the periods in which the magazine is delivered, thus attributing all of the revenue to a single factor — the editorial and publishing activity. Yet, for many magazines the sale of the subscription for cash, is *a*, if not *the*, crucial event. And, if so, some revenue should be recognized at the time of sale.

The amount to be recognized should vary with the degree of confidence in the estimates of future costs. It should also vary inversely with the time expected to elapse before they are incurred. Under certainty, all of the revenue would be recognized at the time of the sale and a liability established for the expected costs (preferably discounted to their present value) of fulfilling the subscription. Much work remains in developing operational guides for allocating revenues to periods. Without such guides, the traditional approach will probably continue: each dollar of cost will be assumed to have earned the same amount of revenue.

If, in a sale on account, collection is expected to be routine, no revenue may be considered earned by the collection function. But if considerable time and effort are expended in effecting a very uncertain collection, revenue should be attributed to the collection function. The absence of market values for such receivables leaves the accountant with little choice but to recognize revenues only as cash is collected, even though the logic of the method may be questioned.

[26] For an indication of possible user support, see Morton Backer, "Financial Reporting and Security Investment Decision," *Financial Executive,* Vol. 34 (December 1966), p. 60.

[27] Concepts and Standards Research Study Committee, *op. cit.,* p. 316. This concept first appeared in John H. Myers, "The Critical Event and the Recognition of Net Profit," *The Accounting Review,* Vol. 34 (October 1959), p. 528. Sprouse and Moonitz, *op. cit.,* p. 47, argue along similar lines, calling for the identification of revenues with the periods in which the major activities necessary to their creation are undertaken.

The American Accounting Association committee on realization suggested three tests of realization: (1) a measurable asset change, (2) a market transaction involving the accounting entity, and (3) the completion of a critical event. Although the critical event may be more appropriately viewed as a substitute for the earning test, application of the idea is likely to bring about an earlier recognition of revenue. The notion of a critical event directs attention away from the routine to the relevant. For example, in "wild-catting" for oil, the critical or relevant event is its discovery. And the relevance of discovery is so great that efforts should be made to record and report it. This may bring about a desirable shift of attention to *relevant* rather than *highly verifiable* data.

Bases of Revenue Recognition[28]

SALES BASIS. Revenue is widely recorded at the time of sale. Because he does not fully know the many ramifications of legal passage of title, the accountant generally accepts delivery with intent to sell as his point of revenue recognition. In many instances, title actually passes on delivery.

Many reasons support revenue recognition at this point. (1) The physical delivery of the goods is a readily discernible event. (2) With passage of title, the risk of loss from price decline or destruction passes to the buyer. (3) The revenue is measurable. (4) The earning process is substantially completed. The sale is often the critical event. (5) Revenue is realized, even in the narrow sense of the receipt of liquid assets since either cash or claims to cash are usually received. (6) With production completed, the expenses of the sale can usually be determined; thus, income can be determined.

The fact that the recorded amounts of revenue may not actually be realized in cash can be satisfactorily treated through the use of allowances for discounts, returns, and uncollectible accounts. Thus, delaying revenue recognition beyond the point of sale is appropriate only when the assets received or the expenses incurred in making the sale cannot be measured. Such circumstances are likely to be rare. The contention that delaying recognition of revenue until time of sale assigns revenue to the wrong period has merit, as discussed below.

CASH COLLECTION BASIS. Recognizing revenue as cash is collected

---

[28]For further discussion, see Grady, *op. cit.*, pp. 76–99; Hendriksen, *op. cit.*, pp. 134–142; Paton and Littleton, *op. cit.*, pp. 50–59.

is generally appropriate only where cash receipt is accompanied by delivery of product or rendering of service—in effect, the sales basis.

Despite critical event theory, the recognition of revenue upon receipt of cash, but prior to delivery of product or rendering of service, is generally rejected in practice. At the same time, delaying the recognition of earned revenue until cash is received is not in accord with the accrual basis of accounting. Consequently, the cash basis of accounting is sanctioned for its expediency, objectivity, and conservatism rather than its theory.

The support in critical event theory for the installment basis of revenue recognition has already been noted. But the installment method is now properly considered unacceptable except where collection of the sales price is not reasonably assured.[29]

Where extreme uncertainty surrounds the ultimate collection of revenues, they should be accounted for under the cost-recovery approach. Here amounts of revenue and expense equal to the cash received in a period are recognized until the entire cost of the sale (or investment) is recovered. All further cash receipts are then entirely income. Such accounting would be proper for cash received from the trustee of the company issuing bonds, some of which were purchased as a speculative investment at a substantial discount from face value plus many years' defaulted accrued interest, regardless of how the payment is described by the trustee.[30]

PRODUCTION BASIS—PRODUCTION IN PROCESS. Recognizing revenue concurrently with the undertaking of the activity which creates it seems to be nearly a theoretic ideal, especially if production is the critical event. This ideal is approached in the accounting for many service revenues, such as interest and rent and those revenues derived from most personal services. The service is usually performed under the terms of a prior agreement. Such performance—the earning process—gives rise to a claim upon the recipient. The revenue is now earned and realized and can even be said to be based upon a market transaction—the original contract. It is properly recorded at this time.

Recording revenue on a percentage-of-completion basis on

---

[29]Grady, *op. cit.,* p. 78. See also Accounting Principles Board, "Omnibus Opinion—1966," *Opinion No. 10* (New York: American Institute of Certified Public Accountants, December 1966), p. 149.

[30]U. S. Securities and Exchange Commission, *Accounting Series Release No. 36,* November 6, 1942.

long-term contracts tends to relate recognition to production. Although critical event theory might call for recognizing some revenue when a successful bid is made on a contract, the only alternative accepted in practice is to recognize revenue when the contract is completed. This alternative approach could lead to the economic inaccuracy of an entity's reporting no revenue or income for a period simply because a contract was not completed, even though the entity's resources were fully employed during that period.

In perhaps most long-term contract situations, the contract price is known and little doubt exists as to its collection. But problems exist in estimating the stage of completion and the total amount of costs expected. The latter may vary widely for uncontrollable reasons (for example, weather) with an effect on net income. Revenue and income are recognized proportionately with completion, which is usually measured by relating costs incurred to total expected costs. The theoretical deficiencies in this approach are that revenue is assumed to be earned as costs are incurred and that each dollar of cost earns the same amount of revenue. Yet, despite these difficulties and deficiencies, the percentage-of-completion approach will probably yield a better description of economic activity than its alternative.

In many industries, the production process consists of the natural growth (timber, livestock) or aging (liquor) of a resource. The term accretion is used to describe these processes. Although the critical event may actually be natural growth, accretion is seldom recognized as revenue until the products are sold. Practical difficulties generally preclude obtaining a verifiable measure of the increase. Even where market values are available for products in intermediate stages of growth (livestock), such values may be considerably less than those expected by the entity for the product when it has matured, less the costs to be incurred to bring the product to maturity.

But accretion is allowed to affect net income in farming, where the natural increase in the livestock owned is inventoried at net market price. These increases are deducted, as a part of the inventory, to determine the cost of the product sold, thus affecting reported net income indirectly.

PRODUCTION BASIS — PRODUCTION COMPLETED. Recognizing revenue upon completion of production is sanctioned in practice for certain precious metals, such as gold and silver, which can be readily sold with no substantial marketing costs at a fixed, government-supported price. For other metals and agricultural products, the requirements are similar but expanded: (1) a stable market price, (2) no substantial marketing costs, (3) interchangeability of units, and (4) difficulty in obtaining approximate actual costs. The need for separate statement of the third requirement can be questioned since it usually is a part of the first. The fourth requirement does not actually justify revenue recognition at this point, but is a condition to be fulfilled if income is to be determined objectively.

Where the above conditions exist, strong theoretical justification supports recognizing revenue upon completion of production. The revenue has been earned—production is the critical event—and the costs of production are likely to be known. The time of revenue recognition is advanced, thereby narrowing the gap between the point of recognition and the expenditure of effort to produce it. Also, the revenue is measurable with a high degree of accuracy. The delivery and selling expenses to be incurred can be estimated with reasonable accuracy since their incurrence is likely to be routine.

Because the accounting unit is not a party to a market transaction, the revenue in the above cases would not be considered realized under the tests for realization advocated by the Concepts and Standards Research Study Committee. On the other hand, Sprouse and Moonitz go further and advocate recognition of revenue in all cases where a ready market exists for a product and where marketing and disposal costs are nominal and predictable.[31]

Summary of Revenue Recognition

Revenue is the product of the entity measured in terms of its exchange value. Generally, it is recognized only after the activities required to produce it have been completed and its ultimate realizable amount is measurable with reasonable accuracy.

In most instances, practical difficulties preclude recognizing revenue concurrently with productive activities. Consequently, revenue is considered earned when substantially all such activities are completed. A substitute idea calls for considering revenue earned when the event most critical to its production has been completed.

The bulk of business revenue is recognized under the view that realization occurs when a sale has been made and liquid assets

[31]*Op. cit.,* p. 47.

received. Other definitions stress the occurrence of a market transaction and the receipt of measurable assets. Exceptions to the general rule are found where revenue is recognized as cash is collected, as production progresses, and when production is completed. The accountant's approach to revenue recognition, therefore, controls the nature and the measurement of certain assets reported.

EXPENSE RECOGNITION

Expense Defined

Expense is the flow of resources or service potentials consumed in the production of the net product of the entity — its revenues. It is defined in nonmonetary terms to distinguish clearly its nature from its measurement.[32] But since service potentials are assets and the seeking of revenue is deliberate and planned, expense is defined as asset expirations voluntarily incurred to produce revenue. By contrast, losses are involuntary asset expirations not related to the production of revenue.

ASSETS DEFINED. With the definition of expense tied to asset expirations, a definition of assets is called for. Basically, assets are service potentials — that is, future benefits.[33] To be of future benefit, these service potentials must not have expired, must have a positive value, and must accrue to a specific entity which has an enforceable claim such that it can exclude others from using or receiving them.[34] Although some definitions of assets include the requirements that they result from a past transaction,[35] or be acquired at a cost,[36] the essential and relevant attributes are the existence of service potential and the right to receive it.

---

[32] Hendriksen, *op. cit.*, p. 143.

[33] *Accounting and Reporting Standards for Corporate Financial Statements, op. cit.*, p. 3. The notions of property right and value acquired are stressed in *Accounting Terminology Bulletin No. 1*, in *Accounting Research and Terminology Bulletins*, Final Edition (New York: American Institute of Certified Public Accountants, 1961), para. 26.

[34] Hendriksen, *op. cit.*, pp. 194–195.

[35] Sprouse and Moonitz, *op. cit.*, p. 8.

[36] Thomas Henry Sanders, Henry Rand Hatfield, and Underhill Moore, *A Statement of Accounting Principles* (New York: American Institute of Accountants, 1938), p. 58.

Expenses have been defined as utilized and lost costs[37] or as expired costs.[38] These definitions undoubtedly stem from the tendency to define assets as unexpired or deferred costs. But such definitions of asset are conceptually inadequate because they focus on the measurement of assets rather than on their service potentials.

EXPENSE INCLUSIONS. Losses are conceptually distinguishable from expenses and should, therefore, be excluded from a determination of net operating income. But because they affect the well-being of an entity, they are properly deductible from revenues in arriving at periodic net income.

Because net income is unchanged, expenses are not differentiated in current practice from revenue modifications, although proper valuation of the assets received would indicate clearly that no asset expired as a result of an uncollectible account or the taking of a sales discount.

Because interest is more a reward for the use of capital than a cause of revenue, a strong case can be built in entity theory for defining it as a distribution rather than a determinant of income.[39] Deduction of interest from revenue as an expense seems appropriate only under proprietary theory. It is also urged that income taxes are not expenses but distributions of income and it is specifically noted that they are not levied in loss years. But here again the measurement of expense is apparently confused with its nature. The entity undoubtedly received services from the governmental unit involved even though there may be no objective or meaningful way to measure them.

The cost of securing capital by issuing stock is usually netted against the proceeds received on the grounds that only the net receipts can be invested in resources. Also, it is alleged that the relationship between such costs, even when capitalized and amortized, and revenues is not cause and effect. But, by the same line of reasoning, should the costs incurred to prepare and issue periodic dividend checks be viewed as expenses? If not, what are they?

[37] H. A. Finney and Herbert E. Miller, *Principles of Accounting–Intermediate*, 6th Ed. (Englewood Cliffs, N. J.: Prentice-Hall, Inc., 1965), p. 146.

[38] *Accounting and Reporting Standards for Corporate Financial Statements, op. cit.*, p. 5. See also Accounting Terminology Bulletin No. 4, para. 3, in *Accounting Research and Terminology Bulletins, op. cit.*

[39] *Accounting and Reporting Standards for Corporate Financial Statements, op. cit.*, p. 5.

Because such costs are necessary to business operations, an indirect relationship with revenues should be assumed and the costs treated as expenses.

The practitioner for the most part tends to disregard these distinctions between losses, revenue modifications, income distributions, and expenses. All deductions necessary to arrive at net income to stockholders are expenses and, while perhaps theoretically deficient, such an approach has the practical advantage of focusing upon an important residual. And while the income statement he prepares shows expenses classified and listed usually in the order of cost of goods sold, selling expenses, administrative expenses, and taxes, all expenses are homogeneous as deductions from revenue. There are no priorities in order of recovery.[40]

Expense Measurement

Ideally, expense measurements should be expressed in terms of the value to the owner of the service potentials consumed in producing revenue. This follows naturally from the notions that the conceptually superior basis of asset valuation is the asset's value to its owner and that expenses are expired assets. This value to the owner is generally conceived to be the present worth of the future net cash receipts expected from it. Because of their subjectivity, expense measurements are discussed largely in terms of some concept of current cost or value or historical cost.

CURRENT COST OR VALUE.   The major arguments for replacement cost have been presented in Chapter 4. But it may also be noted that replacement cost is supported on the grounds that the value of an asset to its owner cannot exceed the cost of replacing it.[41] Presumably, if the present value of an asset is greater than the cost to acquire it, additional assets will be acquired, provided they are sufficiently divisible into small increments, until the two amounts are equal.

The current selling price of an asset, less disposal costs, if any, is supported as a basis of asset valuation because (1) it represents

[40] Paton and Littleton, *op. cit.,* p. 67.

[41] G. Edward Philips, "The Revolution in Accounting Theory," *The Accounting Review,* Vol. 38 (October 1963), p. 707. For a full discussion of this topic, see David Solomons, "Economic and Accounting Concepts of Cost and Value," in *Modern Accounting Theory,* Morton Backer, ed. (Englewood Cliffs, N. J.: Prentice-Hall, Inc., 1966), pp. 122–125.

the value of the asset to its owner in the sense of command over goods and services, (2) it may be the opportunity cost of the asset and thus represent the actual economic sacrifice made when the asset is consumed in the production of revenue, provided other more valuable uses are not available, and (3) it represents the asset's minimum value to its owner. The use of market values is generally rejected because such values do not exist for many assets and the liquidation point of view implicit in their use conflicts with the going-concern concept. But, on occasion, inventory items and other assets removed from service and awaiting sale are valued at their net realizable value.

Of course, an asset may have a value to its owner less than replacement cost but greater than net realizable value. This would be true for assets rendered obsolete by technological change. Such assets may be used to produce goods which can be sold at a profit while the assets themselves may have no or even a negative value — disposition costs may exceed selling price. Thus, apparently there is no single, substitute measure which is at all times and under all conditions the best approximation of present value as determined by discounting expected net future cash receipts.[42]

As noted in Chapter 4, the practitioner generally rejects replacement cost as a basis of asset and expense measurement. But exceptions are recognized, especially where measurements in current terms are most likely to vary substantially from recorded measurements. For example, accelerated depreciation is supported on the grounds that it compensates, at least in part, for the expected higher costs of replacing the assets exhausted. Also, LIFO inventory technique often actually matches replacement cost against recorded revenues.

COST. Although the common practice of measuring expense in terms of historical cost is often justified on grounds of objectivity, some theoretical support may exist. A rational person will not pay more for an asset than he thinks it is worth. At the same time he will expand his purchases of an asset until the value of the marginal unit (and thus the value of all units) is equal to the price paid for it. But when assets can be added only in large units (a blast furnace), the last unit is likely to have a value to its owner greater than its

---

[42] Kenneth W. Lemke, "Asset Valuation and Income Theory," *The Accounting Review*, Vol. 41 (January 1966), p. 34.

cost.[43] This inequality can be narrowed to a certain extent by acquiring assets having greater capacity or quality, such as a larger or a heavy duty truck.

But historical cost is not usually supported because it may approximate value. The primary purpose of accounting is reporting the stewardship of a corporation's management to stockholders.[44] And a properly drawn report on stewardship shows the stockholders' investment as it is committed or embodied in resources and traces these commitments and embodiments as they flow through an entity to outsiders. Thus, the accountant is urged to be concerned with the investment or costs embodied in resources rather than their value.

But, since management's objective is to bring about a growth in value, it would seem that its effectiveness should be appraised in value terms. And the accountant's concern over value is demonstrated by his practices of writing assets down to lower market values and of recording at fair value assets acquired without cost. He also usually records assets at their cost in terms of cash or its equivalent, which is another way of saying they are recorded at their current exchange value. But the cost concept is so deeply embedded in accounting that even assets acquired as gifts are said to have a cost equal to their fair market value at time of receipt.

When an individual asset is acquired for an immediate cash outlay, there is usually little question about its cost. But objective measurement is not always possible. To illustrate: (1) When a group of assets is purchased for a single total price, there is often no nonarbitrary way of assigning the purchase price to the individual assets acquired. (2) There is usually no objective way to determine when a cost has become so excessive as to warrant treating it as a loss rather than a cost — repairs to a vandalized building under construction, for example. (3) When an asset is acquired under terms calling for delayed payment, unless the cash price is stated separately, the interest implicit in the transaction can seldom be separated objectively. (4) The price paid for an asset may not be an objective measure of cost if not bargained for at arm's-length. (5) Where assets are self-constructed, questions may arise as to how much fixed overhead should be charged to the assets, especially

---

[43] Solomons, *op. cit.*, pp. 125–126.

[44] Herman W. Bevis, *Corporate Financial Reporting in a Competitive Economy* (New York: The Macmillan Company, 1965), p. 19.

since such construction is not usually undertaken unless some idle capacity is expected.

The Time of Expense Recognition

When should monetary measurements of the service potentials consumed in producing revenue be charged to expense? The matching principle of accounting provides the answer.

THE MATCHING PRINCIPLE.   Essentially the notion of matching requires that revenues and the expenses incurred to produce them be given concurrent periodic recognition in the accounts. Only if effort (expense) is properly related to accomplishment (revenue) will the difference (income) have any significance as an indicator of efficiency in the use of resources. Thus, the matching principle is a recognition of the cause and effect relationship that exists between expense and revenue.[45]

As already discussed, considerable theoretical support exists for recognizing revenue as the activity undertaken to create it occurs. In this approach, the service potentials consumed in producing revenue, such as raw materials and direct labor services, would be treated as expenses when used. There would be no need to delay recognition of any expense or to hold that the costs of such services somehow attach to the product produced and serve as a measure of its service potential. But revenue recognition is delayed by adherence to the realization principle. And because expense and revenue are to be matched, it follows that the notion of realization also controls, at least to a certain extent, the time of expense recognition. Stated more broadly, expense recognition is theoretically a function of revenue recognition.

But unfortunately lacking is the clearly discernible positive correlation between expense and revenue,[46] which is needed to permit use of this principle as an operational guide. Although necessary to the operations of a business, many expenses simply do not have a discernible relationship to revenues. As a result, the less exact notions of product and period costs have served as rough guides to expense recognition.

[45] Concepts and Standards Research Study Committee, "The Matching Concept," *The Accounting Review*, Vol. 40 (April 1965), pp. 368–372. Matching is referred to as a basic process in income determination by the APB; see Accounting Principles Board, "Accounting for Income Taxes," *Opinion No. 11* (New York: American Institute of Certified Public Accountants, 1967), p. 160.

[46] *Ibid.*, p. 369.

PRODUCT COSTS. Certain factors of production—service potentials—are essential to the production of goods. When measured in terms of cost, these service potentials are called product costs. Once a cost is determined to be a product cost, it is related to specific goods and is expensed when the revenue from the sale of the goods is recognized.

It is generally conceded that fairly accurate approximations of the raw material and direct labor components of product cost can be secured, although arbitrary allocations may be necessary in the case of joint products. Indirect manufacturing costs (overhead) can be related to products only via an allocation process. The usual approach is to allocate a part of the cost of every factor of production necessary to the production of goods to each unit of good produced. This approach—absorption costing—is rejected by the supporters of direct costing. Under direct costing, only the variable costs of production are inventoried as product costs, while fixed production costs are expensed as incurred.[47]

The strongest point in favor of direct costing is that the fixed production costs of one period do not represent service potentials and should not be inventoried and carried forward as assets into a subsequent period if all of the goods which can be sold in this subsequent period can be produced in the period of sale. Under such circumstances, the fixed production costs of the first period can in no way benefit the revenues of the second, or so it is argued. But this may not be true. Production processes are not turned on and off with a flick of the switch. Consequently, inventories must be maintained to prevent loss of sales. Also, lower costs may be obtained from larger production runs, which necessitate carrying inventories.[48] Thus, a better view is that management seeks to act in a prudent, optimal manner, and carrying inventories usually reflects this.

DIRECT, NONPRODUCT COSTS. Occasionally, costs may be specifically related to certain revenues but not to the goods sold. The best example is a salesman's commission. Such a cost should not be expensed in the period incurred, even if the obligation to

---

[47] For further discussion, see James M. Fremgren, "The Direct Costing Issue—An Identification of Issues," *The Accounting Review,* Vol. 39 (January 1964), pp. 43–51.

[48] George H. Sorter and Charles T. Horngren, "Asset Recognition and Economic Attributes—The Relevant Costing Approach," *The Accounting Review,* Vol. 37 (July 1962), p. 398.

pay arises because an order is obtained, if the order is not filled until a subsequent period.

Similarly, a fairly close relationship can be established between costs incurred to promote a new product and the revenues resulting from such product sales. Such costs should not be expensed until revenues from product sales are recognized. Although a question may arise as to the proper period of amortization of such costs, the expensing of such costs in accordance with expected revenue would bring about the desired matching of effort and accomplishment.

In certain instances, costs directly related to specific revenues are incurred subsequent to the period of sale—"after costs" as they are often called. Warranty fulfillment and collection costs are examples. For warranties, revenue is typically recognized at sale and a proper matching secured by accruing the estimated warranty costs to be incurred as expenses of the period of sale. The alternative is to delay recognition of a part of the revenue until the warranty fulfillment costs are incurred and thus assign some revenue to the period in which it is earned by fulfilling the warranty.[49] Collection costs expected to be incurred can also be accrued as expenses of the period of sale, with the alternative—in unusual circumstances—of delaying revenue recognition until cash is collected, where collection costs are expected to be substantial and collection is highly uncertain.

PERIOD COSTS.   When the cost of seeking revenue cannot be related to any specific revenue it is called a period cost. Period costs are expensed in the period incurred. Typically, they are found only in the selling and administrative functions of a business entity, except when direct costing is employed.

Paton and Littleton hold that under ideal circumstances all costs would be attached to products and expensed when the revenue from their sale is recognized.[50] Because all costs cannot be discernibly related to products, certain expenses are matched against revenues on the basis of time periods. But time period matching is an expedient, not the ideal. Implementation of the Paton and

[49] W. A. Paton, "Premature Revenue Recognition," *The Journal of Accountancy,* Vol. 96 (October 1953), pp. 432–437.

[50] *Op. cit.,* p. 15. For a thorough discussion of the period versus product cost controversy, see William Joseph Schrader, *A Critical Evaluation of Income Measurement by "Products" and by "Periods,"* Industrial Research Bulletin No. 6 (University Park, Pa.: Bureau of Business Research, Pennsylvania State University, 1959).

Littleton ideal would require passing all costs through an inventory account and recognizing them as an entity's only expense — cost of goods sold.

Yet the period cost concept would seem to be an expedient only because the recognition of revenue is governed by another expedient — realization. When revenue is recognized as it is created (in a value-added sense), all costs related to its production are period costs. The notion of period costs is then the theoretically supportable idea, and the product cost concept becomes nothing more than a functional classification like selling and administrative costs.

Thus, a natural consequence of the accountant's attempt to reduce uncertainty in revenue measurements by relying upon realization is an increase in the uncertainty surrounding the measurement of periodic expense. And this uncertainty tends to be reflected in most of the reasons that justify the period cost concept:

1. Many costs incurred in a period relate so completely to that period's revenues that satisfactory matching is secured by expensing them as incurred — for example, the weekly newspaper advertisement of the local supermarket.

2. Other costs may bear no relationship to any revenue, yet cannot be avoided if the business is to operate. Such costs are expensed as incurred. For many entities, the cost of the annual audit falls within this classification.

3. Yet other costs, definitely incurred with the expectation that they will influence future revenues, are expensed as incurred for one or both of two reasons: (1) the benefits expected are so uncertain that they cannot be measured; (2) even if the benefits are measurable, the amount of cost to be carried over may be estimated only by engaging in arbitrary allocations of joint costs (cost of pure research, contrasted with applied research, is an example).

4. Finally, certain costs are expensed as incurred because they recur, suggesting that no future benefits from any period's costs are to be expected. And further, even if future benefits are expected, no material distortion would result from immediate expensing, except in the first and last years of an entity's life, if the amounts involved are approximately equal each year. Salaries paid to other than factory employees are examples.

For the above types of cost, a positive correlation with current revenues is assumed simply because "no objectively discernible ability to produce future revenues is associated with them."[51] Yet no cost possesses an inherent attribute which requires that it be im-

[51] Concepts and Standards Research Study Committee, "The Matching Concept," *op. cit.,* p. 370.

mediately and always expensed as incurred. Even costs called period costs when the entity is operating must be capitalized in the entity's formative or pre-revenue stage. They cannot be assumed to be the cause of current revenue since there is no current revenue and no attempt has been made to earn any. These costs must, therefore, relate to future revenues.

LOSSES.   No attempt should be made to match losses to specific revenues since, by definition, they are expired service potentials not related to an attempt to produce revenue. Such expired service potentials should be charged against revenues of the period in which they lose their "discernible ability to produce future revenues." [52] And because they represent expired service potential, losses should not be carried forward as assets.

Distinguishing losses from period costs is not an easy matter and is often judgmental. For example, normal, necessary, anticipated, recurring consumptions of service potential are expenses, while abnormal, unnecessary, unanticipated, nonrecurring expirations are losses. The difficulty of drawing such a distinction supports charging both expenses and losses against current revenues with, of course, the distinction disclosed as clearly as possible.

On the other hand, certain service potential expirations may be corrections of prior period expenses; if so, they should be charged directly to retained earnings where material. An example is an assessment of additional income taxes for a prior year. Although specifically ruled out from consideration as a prior period adjustment by *Opinion No. 9*,[53] in many cases a loss recognized at the sale of plant assets might represent a prior period adjustment. Only where the asset would not have been acquired if the loss had been foreseen is the expiration of service potential clearly a loss and not a prior period adjustment.

Summary of Expense Recognition

Although variously defined, expenses are basically asset expirations voluntarily incurred in the attempted production of revenue, while losses are involuntary expirations not related to revenue production. While conceptually distinguishable, losses, revenue modi-

[52] *Ibid.*

[53] Accounting Principles Board, "Reporting The Results of Operations," *Opinion No. 9* (New York: American Institute of Certified Public Accountants, December 1966), para. 24.

fications, and income distributions (interest) often are not, as a practical matter, distinguished from expenses.

Ideally, expenses should be measured in terms of the owner's value of the assets consumed. Some theoretical support exists for the contention that this value may be equal to historical cost when an asset is acquired. But expenses are typically measured in historical cost and justified on grounds of objectivity and appropriateness as a basis for stewardship reporting.

If income is to be an index of efficiency, expenses (efforts) and revenues (accomplishments) must be recognized concurrently. The realization principle delays the recognition of revenue, and the matching principle requires that the recognition of expenses be delayed until revenue is recognized. Because a positive correlation between expense and revenue is often not discernible, the notions of product and period costs are employed to facilitate expense recognition. Product costs are attached to products and expensed when the product is sold. Period costs are expensed as incurred. Losses are recognized in the period incurred.

QUESTIONS

1. (a) Prepare a definition of realization broad enough to embrace the actual revenue recognition practices of business outlined in the chapter. (b) Why might such a definition be of little value?

2. Which of the following cash receipts of the X Corporation during its current year should be reflected as revenue in its income statement for the year? (a) Damages awarded by a court for infringement by a competitor on a patent owned by the X Corporation. (b) The recovery of a relatively large account receivable written off as uncollectible several years ago. (c) An amount received from the publisher of a magazine in settlement of a suit for libel instituted by the X Corporation against the publisher. (d) The proceeds of a substantial life insurance policy on a company executive killed in an accident during the year. (e) The amount by which the settlement received from an insurance company exceeded the book value of assets destroyed by fire.

3. If you were to apply the realization principle that requires changes in assets and liabilities to be recognized as soon as they have become sufficiently definite and objective, what tests would you employ?

4. How can it be argued that certainty in the environment justifies recognizing revenue upon completing production?

5. Does the position that certain costs are period costs to be expensed as

incurred contradict the position that expense recognition is essentially triggered by recognition of revenue? Explain.

6. (a) Has the owner of merchandise regularly held for sale realized revenue when such merchandise is exchanged for office furniture? Explain. (b) Assume that an entity received 100 shares of its own common stock from a customer in exchange for merchandise with a regular selling price of $1,500, which is also the market price of the common stock. The merchandise has a cost of $1,000. Has revenue been realized? Explain.

7. (a) Criticize the following definitions: Assets are deferred costs. Expenses are expired costs. (b) Prepare another title for the asset Research and Development Costs which does not include the basis of measurement of the asset.

8. Currently there is considerable dissatisfaction about how some businesses fulfill product warranties. Does the way costs and revenues associated with such warranties are accounted for contribute to dissatisfaction? Explain.

9. Is the period cost concept consistent with the transactions approach to income measurement? Explain.

10. An entity received and recorded at face value a $100,000, 4 per cent 90-day note accepted upon sale of merchandise to a customer. Fifteen days later the note was discounted at the local bank. Proceeds amounted to $99,837.50. What is the nature of the $162.50 ($100,000 − $99,837.50)? Explain.

11. (a) Of the various times at which revenue might be recognized, which seems theoretically preferable? (b) Which is preferred in practice? Why?

12. What are the theoretical deficiencies in recognizing revenue on a percentage-of-completion basis with percentage of completion determined by the amount of costs incurred relative to total expected costs?

13. What apparently are the upper and lower limits to the value of an asset to its owner? Explain.

14. "The matching principle tends only to undo the damage caused by adhering to the realization principle." (a) What does this statement mean? (b) Do you agree? Explain.

15. (a) What are the conceptual bases for distinguishing between expenses and losses? (b) Why should such a distinction be drawn? (c) Why doesn't the practicing accountant strive vigorously to draw this distinction?

16. The amount of uncollectible accounts receivable has been variously referred to in accounting as a loss, an expense, or as a sales adjustment. (a) Present the theoretical arguments pro and con each of these classi-

fications. (b) State which classification seems theoretically correct to you and why.

17. It has been contended that cash discounts are (1) granted to increase the total demand for the seller's goods, (2) incurred in lieu of collection costs, and (3) substitutes for the interest that would be incurred if the granting of cash discounts did not bring about the quick collection of the accounts. (a) State the accounting treatment of discounts implied in each of the above arguments. (b) Discuss the theoretical merits of each of these accounting treatments.

18. You are the auditor for a firm just completing its first year of operation. Many of the costs incurred during the year have been expensed as period costs, with a resulting substantial loss. The president of the company argues that the loss should be capitalized since many of the first year expenses will actually benefit future years. He specifically cites advertising, employee training costs, employee recruitment costs, and research and development costs. He also argues that the loss should be capitalized since it was expected and that the present value of the expected future receipts is greater than the recorded investment in the business plus the first year's loss. (a) Discuss the president's contention that the loss should be capitalized because many of the costs expensed will benefit future periods. (b) Do the president's contentions that the loss was anticipated or that the present value of the expected cash receipts is greater than the recorded investment in the business justify capitalizing the loss? Explain.

19. In completing a very substantial plant modernization program, the Ace Corporation retired a substantial amount of depreciable assets, incurring rather heavy removal and demolition costs. The balance sheet prepared at the end of the year in which this activity occurred showed an asset entitled Deferred Plant Modernization Costs of $3 million. A footnote to the balance sheet shows the computation of this amount as follows:

Cost of assets retired	$20,000,000
Accumulated depreciation	15,000,000
Net book value	$ 5,000,000
Removal and demolition costs	1,000,000
Total	$ 6,000,000
Less: Tax effect (50% rate)	3,000,000
Deferred plant modernization costs	$ 3,000,000

The note further explains that the entire $6 million was written off for tax purposes during the year, but since it was capitalized for financial reporting purposes, tax allocation procedures were applied. The $3 million is to be amortized over the next five years. Present your appraisal of the theoretical soundness of the company's accounting for the above items.

20. Electronics, Incorporated is a retailer of television sets, radios, stereo and hi fi equipment and components, and other electrical appliances. It also services all types of such merchandise. On the last day of its accounting period, it sold a color television set for $700 cash. Included in the sale is a one-year service contract which the company would sell to anyone possessing a new color television set for $100. The cost of the set sold is $450 and the estimated cost of servicing the set for the coming year is $70.

    Indicate two alternative procedures to account for the above and state the theoretical justification supporting each.

21. The owner of Health Studios, Inc. has asked your advice on a revenue recognition problem. The company sells life memberships in a health club (the contract legally guarantees a minimum membership period of seven years). The club provides a place for exercising, various types of exercise equipment, a swimming pool, a steamroom, a sunroom, a mineral whirlpool, showers, and lockers. Three salaried employees provide guidance and establish exercise programs for the club members. The major costs incurred in operating the club are building and equipment depreciation and taxes, employee salaries, utilities, insurance, repairs and maintenance, and cleaning.

    Memberships in the club are sold for $330 cash or on an installment contract basis calling for 24 monthly payments of $15.50. All such contracts are sold immediately to a local bank for $330 cash. The salaried employee selling the contract receives a commission of $50. Club records show that several members who joined over four years ago when the club was first organized still exercise regularly. In other cases, a member appears regularly for three or four weeks and then is seldom seen again, although his privileges continue. In nearly one-half of the cases, appearance at the club becomes quite sporadic after one year. No refunds are available to members wishing to surrender their memberships, and the memberships are not transferable. The entire amount received on the sale of memberships is taxable income at receipt.

    (a) Outline for the owner of Health Studios, Inc. the alternative approaches to revenue recognition for the above circumstances.

    (b) Evaluate each of these approaches carefully. (Hints: What accounting treatment would critical event theory suggest? Have you carefully matched costs and revenues?)

6

PRINCIPLES, ALTERNATIVES, AND UNIFORMITY

Regardless of the approach taken in attempting to erect a structure of accounting theory, principles are important. Discussed first in this chapter are the two most recent attempts, both sponsored by the AICPA, to discover and state the principles of accounting. The controversy surrounding the first of these attempts and the loose and sometimes contradictory nature of the principles presented in the second tend to reinforce a lesson that should have been learned from over 20 years of experience—progress in stating the principles of accounting comes slowly.[1] Attention is next directed to the uniformity-diversity controversy. That uniformity should become the topic of recent debate is undoubtedly due to (1) the concern of some that the APB might seek to require adherence to a body of uniform principles, (2) the growing number of alternatives considered acceptable in practice, and (3) increasing user awareness of the possible and actual lack of comparability in financial information resulting from the employment of accounting alternatives.

Accounting Research Study No. 3

When, as discussed in Chapter 2, the AICPA through its governing council adopted a new research program in 1959, the initial assignment given to its research division was to study the basic postulates and broad principles of accounting. *Accounting Research*

---

[1] Reed K. Storey, *The Search for Accounting Principles* (New York: American Institute of Certified Public Accountants, 1964), p. 60.

Study No. 1 and *No. 3* were submitted to the Accounting Principles Board in fulfillment of that assignment.[2]

NEGATIVE REACTION.   In 1962 the Board noted the considerable reaction, largely negative,[3] to *ARS No. 3* in a "Statement by the Accounting Principles Board." By implying that broad principles can be distinguished from generally accepted accounting principles, the Board left the impression that a structured theory of accounting should consist of basic postulates, broad principles (such as, perhaps, realization and matching), and generally accepted accounting principles (such as the more specific directives in the *Accounting Research Bulletins*). It also found the ideas contained in *ARS No. 1* and *No. 3* "too radically different from present generally accepted accounting principles for acceptance at this time."

REASONS FOR REJECTION.   There are probably many reasons why the Board found these studies "too radically different." [4] Undoubtedly included are (1) the recommendation that inventories be valued at net realizable value, if objectively determinable, otherwise at replacement cost; (2) the recommendation that plant assets be periodically revalued at replacement cost; (3) the general emphasis upon values rather than the more traditional costs-attach doctrine; (4) the discarding of the principle of realization as a necessary corollary to the above three recommendations; (5) the recommendation that changes in resources be measured and classified according to

---

[2] Maurice Moonitz, "The Basic Postulates of Accounting," *Accounting Research Study No. 1* (New York: American Institute of Certified Public Accountants, 1961); Robert T. Sprouse and Maurice Moonitz, "A Tentative Set of Broad Accounting Principles for Business Enterprises," *Accounting Research Study No. 3* (New York: American Institute of Certified Public Accountants, 1962).

[3] See comments by some of the members of the advisory committees on these two studies in Sprouse and Moonitz, *op. cit.*, pp. 60 ff.

[4] In addition to the reference cited in footnote 3 above, see Harvey T. Deinzer, *Development of Accounting Thought* (New York: Holt, Rinehart and Winston, Inc., 1965), Chaps. 8 and 9; Robert T. Sprouse, "The 'Radically Different' Principles of Accounting Research Study No. 3," *The Journal of Accountancy*, Vol. 118 (May 1964), pp. 63–69; A. C. Littleton's review of "A Tentative Set of Broad Accounting Principles for Business Enterprises," *The Accounting Review*, Vol. 38 (January 1963), pp. 220–222; William J. Vatter, "Postulates and Principles," *The Journal of Accounting Research*, Vol. 1 (Autumn 1963), pp. 179–197; Eric L. Kohler, "Why Not Retain Historical Cost?" *The Journal of Accountancy*, Vol. 116 (October 1963), pp. 35–41; AICPA Staff, "Comments on 'A Tentative Set of Broad Accounting Principles for Business Enterprises,'" *The Journal of Accountancy*, Vol. 115 (April 1963), pp. 36–48.

the amounts resulting from general price level change, changes in replacement cost, efforts made to earn profits, and other causes, such as accretion; (6) the downgrading of conservatism to a position of less importance than many believe it to hold in practice; (7) the heavy emphasis upon the need to discount future amounts payable to their present values; (8) the overemphasis upon theory and logic and the failure to blend in practical considerations; (9) the failure to show that the principles presented meet the needs of interested parties; and (10) the failure to show how the principles espoused follow directly from the postulates presented.

The strong negative response to the principles presented, especially from practitioners, demonstrated clearly that *ARS No. 3* was a normative statement of what the authors thought accounting principles should be rather than what they actually are. This was fully in accord with the charge given the authors. They were expected to provide more than a survey of existing practices.

Since the negative response to *ARS No. 3* made it quite unlikely that it could serve as a basis for a Board pronouncement on principles, the Board chose another approach. Rather than seeking directly to prepare a statement of accounting principles, it authorized (1963) a research project to inventory the principles of current acceptance. The results were published in 1965.[5]

Accounting Research Study No. 7

As the term inventory implies, *ARS No. 7* was undertaken not to discover new or better accounting principles but (1) to present the basic postulates or concepts to which accounting principles are oriented, (2) to enumerate the principles (or practices) currently adhered to or employed by the accountant in fulfilling his financial reporting obligation, and (3) to indicate the authoritative support for such principles—*Accounting Research Bulletins,* Board opinions, SEC rules and regulations, and so on.[6]

THE PRINCIPLES OF ARS NO. 7.   This presents five major objectives of accounting and the principles to be adhered to in order to attain them. The 32 principles are reproduced below in their entirety except for minor omissions indicated by an asterisk.

[5]Paul Grady, "Inventory of Generally Accepted Accounting Principles for Business Enterprises," *Accounting Research Study No. 7* (New York: American Institute of Certified Public Accountants, 1965).

[6]*Ibid.,* p. ix.

Objective A. Account for sales, revenues, income, cost of sales, expenses, gains and losses in such manner as to present fairly the results of operations for the period or periods of time covered.

Principle A-1. Sales, revenues and income should not be anticipated or materially overstated or understated.*

Principle A-2. Costs of sales and expenses should be appropriately matched against the periodic sales and revenues.*

Principle A-3. Appropriate charges should be made for depreciation and depletion of fixed assets and for amortization of other deferred costs.

Principle A-4. Proper distribution of costs should be made as between fixed assets, inventories, maintenance and expense.*

Principle A-5. Contingency provisions and reserves should not be misused as a means of arbitrarily reducing income or shifting income from one period to another.

Principle A-6. Nonrecurring and extraordinary gains and losses should be recognized in the period they occur, but should be shown separately from the ordinary and usual operations.

Principle A-7. There is a strong presumption that all gains and losses will be included in periodic income statements unless they are of such magnitude in relation to revenues and expenses from regular operations as to cause the statements to be misleading.

Principle A-8. Disclose rental charges under material leases and capitalize those which are in effect installment purchases of fixed assets.

Principle A-9. If accounting principles in the determination of periodic results have not been consistently maintained, the effect of the change should be stated.

Objective B. Account for the equity capital invested by stockholders through contribution of assets or retained earnings in a meaningful manner on a cumulative basis and as to changes during the period or periods covered. The account structure and presentation in financial statements of a business entity are designed to meet statutory and corporate charter requirements and to portray significant financial relationships.

Principle B-1. In case there are two or more classes of stock, account for the equity capital invested for each and disclose the rights and preferences to dividends and to principal in liquidation.

Principle B-2. From a financial viewpoint the capital invested by stockholders is the corpus of the enterprise and its identity should be fully maintained. Any impairment of invested capital resulting from operating deficits, losses of any nature, dividend distributions in excess of earnings, and treasury stock purchases is accounted for both currently and cumulatively.

Principle B-3. Capital surplus, however created, should not be used to relieve the income account of the current or future years of charges which would otherwise fall to be made thereagainst. There should be no commingling of retained earnings with invested capital in excess of par or stated values.

Principle B-4. Retained earnings should represent the cumulative balance of periodic earnings less dividend distributions in cash, property or stock, plus or minus gains and losses of such magnitude as not to be properly included in periodic earnings. The entire amount may be presumed to be unrestricted as to dividend distributions unless restrictions are indicated in the financial statements.

Principle B-5. Retained earnings may be decreased by transfers to invested capital accounts when formal corporate action has, in fact, changed the composition of the equity capital. Accumulated deficit accounts may be eliminated against invested capital accounts through formal action approved by stockholders, which establishes a new base line of accountability.

Principle B-6. The amount of any revaluation credits should be separately classified in the stockholder's equity section, and it is not available for any type of charge except on reversal of the revaluation.

Principle B-7. Disclose status of stock options to employees or others and changes therein during the period or periods covered.

Objective C. Account for the assets invested in the enterprise by stockholders (through property contributed or retained earnings) and creditors, in a meaningful manner, so that when considered with the liabilities and equity capital of stockholders there will be a fair presentation of the financial position of the enterprise both at the beginning and end of the period. It should be understood that financial position or balance sheet statements do not purport to show either present values of assets to the enterprise or values which might be realized in liquidation.

Principle C-1. Items classified as current assets should be carried at not more than is reasonably expected to be realized within one year or within the normal operating cycle of the particular business. Cash should be segregated between unrestricted and restricted items, and the inclusion of the latter in current assets justified by their nature. Receivables should be reduced by allowance accounts to cover expected collection or other losses. Receivables from officers, employees, or affiliated companies should be shown separately. Inventories should be carried at cost or market, whichever is lower. Cost comprises direct costs plus factory overhead costs, and the basis of determination (e.g., Lifo, Fifo or average) should be stated. Prepaid items should be properly chargeable to future periods.

Principle C-2. Fixed assets should be carried at cost of acquisition or construction in the historical accounts, unless such cost is no longer meaningful. Cost of land should ordinarily be shown separately. Cost of construction includes direct costs and overhead costs incurred, such as engineering, supervision and administration, interest and taxes. Items treated as fixed assets should have at least one year of expected useful life to the enterprise, and normally the life is considerably longer. Items no longer in service should be removed in order that fixed assets will represent the cost of properties in service.

Principle C-3. Appropriate provision or allowance should be made in order to charge operations with the investment in depreciable assets over the estimated life thereof.

Principle C-4. Long-term investments in securities ordinarily should be carried at cost. When market quotations are available, the aggregate quoted amounts should be disclosed. Investments in affiliates should be segregated from other investments.

Principle C-5. The costs of intangible items, such as debt discount and expense, patents, copyrights, research and development (if deferred) and goodwill should be shown separately. Limited-term items should be amortized against earnings over their estimated lives. The policy in regard to amortization of unlimited-term intangibles should be disclosed.

Principle C-6. The nature and extent of hypothecated or pledged assets should be shown.

Objective D. Account for all known liabilities in a meaningful manner in order that their summarization, considered together with the statement of assets and equity invested by stockholders, will fairly present the financial position of the enterprise at the beginning and end of the period.

Principle D-1. All known liabilities should be recorded regardless of whether the definite amount is determinable. If the amounts cannot be reasonably approximated, the nature of the items should be disclosed on the face of the summary of liabilities or by footnote.

Principle D-2. Current liabilities should include items payable within one year or at the end of the operating business cycle used in the classification of current assets.

Principle D-3. Long-term liabilities should be described and due dates and rates of interest shown.

Principle D-4. The nature and extent to which specific liabilities are a preferred lien on assets should be shown.

Principle D-5. Deferred income should be separately classified and described.

Principle D-6. Contingent liabilities of importance should be disclosed.

Objective E. Financial statements should comply with the applicable reporting standards included in generally accepted auditing standards. Reporting to investors should be performed on an entity basis.

Principle E-1. Generally accepted reporting standards applicable to financial statements are set forth in Chapters 7, 8, 9 and 11 of Statements on Auditing Procedure No. 33.

Principle E-2. Where there is a parent company and one or more subsidiaries, there is a presumption that consolidated statements are more meaningful than separate statements.

Principle E-3. The accounts of consolidated subsidiaries or divisions operating in foreign countries should be translated into dollars at the appropriate rates of exchange.

Principle E-4. Where two or more previously independent entities merge or otherwise combine in such a manner as to constitute a pooling of interests, the new entity inherits the bases of accountability of the constituent entities.[7]

[7] *Ibid.*, pp. 57–67.

Principle E-1, in effect, provides the following guides to financial reporting: (1) that the financial statements are to be prepared through adherence to generally accepted accounting principles, (2) that such principles be applied consistently through time, (3) that disclosure in the financial statements is to be regarded as reasonably adequate unless otherwise noted, and (4) that the effects of certain events occurring after the date of the statements but before they are issued be disclosed if necessary for a fair presentation.

ARE THE PRINCIPLES THE PROFESSION'S?   Are the principles in *ARS No. 7* the profession's generally accepted accounting principles? Yes and no. They are if a principle can be defined as a broad, general rule adopted as a guide to action—a guide that can be deviated from.

But are the principles presented accurate generalizations of the variety of current accounting practices? There can be little doubt that the practices discussed are currently employed. They are required or recommended in SEC rules and regulations, *Accounting Research Bulletins,* APB Opinions, etc. That they are employed can be readily discerned from the Institute's *Accounting Trends and Techniques*—an annual survey of the accounting practices of 600 large corporations. And general support for the *ARS No. 7* principles can be found in the literature of accounting.[8]

The task of stating accounting principles broadly enough to embrace existing alternative practices is a difficult one in itself and if accomplished yields several undesirable results. A principle stated broadly enough to embrace contradictory practices will of necessity contain its own contradiction. For example, Principle C-2 requires fixed assets to be valued at cost or not at cost. This provides no guidance since it includes all possibilities.[9] Or, if a principle does not contradict itself, it may be stated in such broad terms and

---

[8] See, for example, Weldon Powell, "Inventory of Generally Accepted Accounting Principles," *The Journal of Accountancy,* Vol. 119 (March 1965), pp. 29–35; "Accounting Research Study No. 7" (editorial), *The Journal of Accountancy,* Vol. 119 (March 1965), p. 27; review by Robert N. Anthony in *The Accounting Review,* Vol. 41 (January 1966), pp. 194–196; E. L. Hicks, "Nature of the Inventory," and T. Edward Hollander, "Long Range Importance of the Inventory," *The New York Certified Public Accountant,* Vol. 25 (October 1965), pp. 761–766; A. C. Littleton, "An Inventory of Principles," *The Illinois CPA,* Vol. 27 (Summer 1965), pp. 14–16. For critical comment, see R. J. Chambers, "A Matter of Principle," *The Accounting Review,* Vol. 41 (July 1966), pp. 443–457.

[9] Chambers, *op. cit.,* p. 447.

so nebulously that it provides no real guidance. For example, to fulfill the objective of presenting the results of operations "fairly," Principle A-1 requires that revenues not be anticipated. The accepted practices of recognizing revenue include recognition at time of cash collection and as a product progresses through various stages of completion. Apparently neither constitutes anticipation of revenue.

The clarity of the principles also suffers from what have been called weasel words.[10] The meaning of such terms is not clear from the context; these words include "proper," "appropriate," "applicable," "meaningful," "arbitrarily," and "ordinarily." And Objective C possesses both weasel words and is contradictory.[11] It directs that assets be accounted for in a meaningful manner to yield a fair presentation and then denies that a balance sheet is to show either the present or liquidation values of those assets.[12] But this is more a question of objectives than alternatives.

Alternatives in Accounting

It is generally believed that measures of financial position and operating results may differ widely according to the way many items are accounted for. But there is little agreement about whether these differences result from alternative concepts, principles, procedures, practices, or rules. Since this semantic issue is dealt with later, the term alternatives is used broadly to describe all variations in the manner in which an accounting may be undertaken.

Two major listings of alternatives are available. The first of these is a memorandum prepared by the Chief Accountant of the SEC for a House of Representatives subcommittee.[13] The second is found in *Accounting Research Study No. 7.*[14]

[10] *Ibid.*, p. 457.

[11] *Ibid.*, p. 447.

[12] For a presentation of the results of a survey to determine whether the respondents believe financial statements to be fair *and* in accordance with generally accepted accounting principles, fair *because* they are in accord with these principles, fair only to the extent that these principles are fair, see Abraham Briloff, *The Effectiveness of Accounting Communication* (New York: Frederick A. Praeger, Publishers, 1967), pp. 16–19.

[13] "Memorandum Prepared by the Office of the Chief Accountant, Securities and Exchange Commission, in Response to Request of the Subcommittee on Commerce and Finance of the Committee on Interstate and Foreign Commerce, House of Representatives, on H. R. 6793," reprinted in Grady, *op. cit.*, pp. 385–397.

[14] *Ibid.*, pp. 373–379.

THE SEC REPORT.   Eight areas of accounting where the use of alternatives could produce materially different results are discussed in this report. These include (1) valuation of inventories, with primary references to LIFO and FIFO; (2) depreciation and depletion; (3) income tax allocation, including the problem of accounting for the investment credit; (4) pensions; (5) research and development costs; (6) goodwill; (7) the question of when revenue and income are realized; and (8) the all-inclusive versus the current operating performance concept of income reporting.

Since publication of this report, the Accounting Principles Board has moved to narrow the range of alternatives in some of these areas. For example, as discussed in Chapter 5, Opinions have been issued recommending discontinuance of the installment sales method of recognizing revenue and that certain items often reported in the retained earnings statement now be reported in the income statement.

Opinion No. 8 has narrowed the range of alternatives in accounting for pensions by ruling out the pay-as-you-go and terminal funding approaches, although many alternatives remain.[15] On the other hand, the Board's proposal to consider only the deferred method of accounting for the investment credit acceptable met with such disagreement that it was stricken from the opinion on which the members of the Board voted.[16] As finally published, *Opinion No. 11* supports comprehensive tax allocation—that is, that taxes be allocated for all material differences between taxable income and reported income before taxes regardless what period might elapse before the differences are reversed.[17] A real test of the Board's ability to limit alternatives may be forthcoming, since several large CPA firms and a number of companies disagree with this position.[18]

---

[15] For further discussion, see the many articles in the August, September, October, and December 1967 issues of *The Journal of Accountancy,* Vol. 124.

[16] "APB Modifies Tax and Omnibus Opinions," *The CPA,* Vol. 47 (December 1967), pp. 1, 10.

[17] Accounting Principles Board, "Accounting for Income Taxes," *Opinion No. 11* (New York: American Institute of Certified Public Accountants, December 1967).

[18] Price Waterhouse & Co., *Is Generally Accepted Accounting for Income Taxes Possibly Misleading Investors?* (New York: Price Waterhouse & Co., 1967); Richard T. Baker, "Accounting Is Being Challenged: Needed—A Timely Answer," Address at the Sixth Annual Accounting Forum of Hayden, Stone, Incorporated, November 10, 1967 (privately published); "Survey of Current Practices in Accounting for Investment Tax Credit and in Allocating Income Taxes," *Financial Executive,* Vol. 35 (September 1967), pp. 79–80, 88.

Further attempts to limit alternatives should occur in the near future, since research projects are under way on a number of topics, including—among those in the above SEC report—goodwill and research development costs.

ARS NO. 7 ALTERNATIVES. *ARS No. 7* contains a long list of accounting alternatives in addition to those cited in the SEC report. The list is not claimed to be all-inclusive. Nor are the alternatives listed all of the same nature. In some instances management is free to choose, while in others choice is conditioned by underlying circumstances.

Some of the additional areas where accounting alternatives are employed and the number of alternatives considered acceptable are (1) cash discounts on sales, 2; (2) excise taxes, 2; (3) real and personal property taxes, 8; (4) dividends on common shares payable in common shares, 2; (5) investments in unconsolidated subsidiaries, 2; (6) bases at which plant assets are recorded when acquired, 4; (7) bases of recording self-constructed assets, 3; (8) losses on plant assets, 2; (9) development costs in extractive industries, 3; (10) leases, 2; (11) fire losses, 2; and (12) business combinations, 2.[19]

On the surface it would appear that a total of 31 areas are cited, for which some 80 alternatives are recognized. But such appearances may be deceiving. For example, the four basic approaches to inventory measurement cited do not include the bases of standard cost, lower-of-cost-or-market, and market value. Nor does this total include all combinations of methods—FIFO or average cost in the lower-of-cost-or-market method, for example—the alternative ways of determining market, or the alternative ways of applying the method. Nor does it include the alternative valuations resulting from the exclusion from inventory of varying items of manufacturing overhead. The possible alternative combinations for inventory alone are infinite.[20]

But Grady is not perturbed by the number or the existence of alternatives. He argues that alternatives, especially those applicable or not depending on circumstances, are needed "to prevent financial and accounting abuses."[21] In the light of existing practices one

[19] Grady, *op. cit.*, pp. 373–379.
[20] For further discussion, see Chambers, *op. cit.*, p. 455.
[21] Grady, *op. cit.*, p. 373.

might contend that the above quotation would be more truly descriptive if "encourage" were substituted for "prevent."

Effects of Alternatives

Because the financial press has reported the differing opinions of accountants, users of financial statements have become more knowledgeable about possible accounting alternatives. To a lesser degree they have also become knowledgeable about the actual dollar effect of switching from one accounting alternative to another.[22] Such disclosures are required by generally accepted accounting principles. In any event, users know that the information they rely upon may not be truly comparable and that differences may be more apparent than real.

USER REACTION.   User reaction has been virtually unanimous and bitingly critical. Generally accepted accounting principles are called "gobbledygook guides."[23] Others, in discussing reliance upon financial statements, speak of a "crisis in confidence"[24] and a "credibility gap."[25] An editorial in *Forbes* demanded that the accountant be held responsible for practices which can be used to conceal rather than reveal financial position.[26]

Users have responded in a more forceful way. They have brought over 50 lawsuits against members of the eight largest American CPA firms, seeking to recover damages from alleged irregularities and negligence in the preparation and presentation of financial statements.[27] The threat is that if the accounting profession cannot put its house in order, legislatures must.

---

[22] For some examples, see Thomas F. Keller, "Uniformity versus Flexibility: A Review of the Rhetoric," and Charles E. Johnson, "Management and Accounting Principles," *Law and Contemporary Problems,* Vol. 30 (Autumn 1965), pp. 636–651 and 690–705 (this entire issue of this periodical is devoted to uniformity in financial accounting). See also Robert T. Sprouse, "Observations Concerning the Realization Concept," *The Accounting Review,* Vol. 40 (July 1965), pp. 522–526, and his "Accounting For-What-You-May-Call-Its," *The Journal of Accountancy,* Vol. 122 (October 1966), pp. 45–53.

[23] "CPA Audits and Gobbledygook Guides," *Wall Street Journal,* June 7, 1967, p. 16.

[24] "Crisis in Confidence," *Barron's,* April 10, 1967, pp. 5, 18–19.

[25] "What Are Earnings? The Growing Credibility Gap," *Forbes,* May 15, 1967, p. 32.

[26] As quoted in Briloff, *op. cit.,* p. ix.

[27] "What Are Earnings? The Growing Credibility Gap," *op. cit.,* pp. 31–32.

THE DOLLAR EFFECTS OF ALTERNATIVES.   One of the major obstacles to empirical research in accounting is the lack of knowledge of the dollar effects of alternatives. Seldom is such information released or are researchers able to unearth it for any substantial periods of time.[28] This paucity of information is attested to rather authoritatively. In a hearing held by a House of Representatives subcommittee in 1964, the chairman of the SEC was asked if he would present a report indicating, among other things, the impact of the various accounting alternatives. Andrew Barr, the Chief Accountant of the Commission, advised his chairman that they would find it difficult to measure the effects of such alternatives.[29] If the impact of accounting alternatives cannot be evaluated by the SEC with its information and competent staff, such an evaluation probably cannot be readily secured anywhere.

Lacking empirical evidence, accountants have constructed examples of hypothetical companies assumed to be identical in all respects except that substantial differences in earnings per share emerge solely from the accounting alternatives employed.[30] The differences in earnings per share are then made to reflect stock prices by assuming that the stock of companies in the same industry will sell at roughly the same price-earnings ratio. As discussed below, this assumption may not be valid.

This insufficiency of data has also led researchers to attempt to determine, through simulation techniques, the effects of accounting alternatives upon the price buyers might pay for an entire business.[31] And further research has been undertaken to determine whether

[28] For some exceptions, see John L. Fox, " 'Useful Comparability' in Financial Reporting," *The Journal of Accountancy*, Vol. 118 (December 1964), pp. 44–52; Nicholas Dopuch and David F. Drake, "The Effect of Alternative Accounting Rules for Nonsubsidiary Investments," *Empirical Research in Accounting: Selected Studies, 1966* (Chicago: Institute of Professional Accounting, University of Chicago, 1967), pp. 193–219; Myron J. Gordon, Bertrand N. Horwitz, Philip T. Meyers, "Accounting Measurements and Normal Growth of the Firm," in *Research in Accounting Measurement*, Robert K. Jaedicke, Yuji Ijiri, Oswald Nielsen, eds. (Evanston, Ill.: American Accounting Association, 1966), pp. 221–231; Price Waterhouse & Co., *op. cit.*

[29] Briloff, *op. cit.*, p. 34.

[30] For an evaluation of such an example, see Leonard M. Savoie, "Accounting Improvement: How Fast, How Far?" *Harvard Business Review*, Vol. 41 (July-August 1963), pp. 144–160.

[31] Thomas R. Dyckman, "On the Effects of Earnings-Trend, Size and Inventory Valuation Procedures in Evaluating a Business Firm," *Research in Accounting Measurement, op. cit.*, pp. 175–185.

a corporation has a personality and, if so, whether it might consistently adopt alternatives yielding "conservative" reported information.[32]

THE QUALITY OF EARNINGS. Financial analysts, aware of but unable to quantify the effects of accounting alternatives, attempt to take them into consideration by determining the quality of earnings.[33] Although used rather loosely, the basic implication in the term is that in determining stock values a higher multiplier should be applied to high-quality than to low-quality earnings.[34]

Thus, other things equal, the earnings of a company using conservative accounting alternatives — LIFO, accelerated depreciation — are deemed to be of higher quality and value than a like amount of earnings reported by a company using less conservative alternatives. The quality of earnings is also affected by other factors, such as their stability, growth pattern, and source — geographic or product line.

Evaluating the effects of accounting alternatives in this manner is obviously crude. How much, for example, should the multiplier be increased because of the use of LIFO? The question then arises: Is there a better approach? Since release on a continuing basis of the effects of alternatives seems neither economically feasible, politically desirable, nor practically possible, the indicated solution is the elimination of alternatives in accounting. The feasibility of this solution is discussed below.

THE UNIFORMITY-DIVERSITY CONTROVERSY

Widespread belief exists that comparability of financial information is dependent upon uniformity in accounting. And the extent

[32] George H. Sorter, Selwyn W. Becker, T. Ross Archibald, and William H. Beaver, "Accounting and Financial Measures as Indicators of Corporate Personality — Some Empirical Findings," *Research in Accounting Measurement, op. cit.,* pp. 200–210.

[33] The term "quality of earnings" was used repeatedly by Richard R. Jeffrey, Director of Research, Ford Foundation, in discussions at the symposium on "The Use of Accounting Data in External Decision Making" sponsored by the Accounting Department of the Ohio State University and held on the OSU campus on April 14, 1966. See also Douglas A. Hayes, "Accounting Principles and Investment Analysis," *Law and Contemporary Problems, op. cit.,* p. 761.

[34] For an empirical study, see John L. O'Donnell, "Relationships between Reported Earnings and Stock Prices in the Electric Utility Industry," *The Accounting Review,* Vol. 40 (January 1965), pp. 135–143.

to which the accounting undertaken by nonregulated business entities can and should be uniform is truly controversial.[35] Although
dealt with by an Institute committee as early as 1917, uniformity
became a modern controversy after the Institute in 1959 included
among its responsibilities the advancement of the written expression
of accounting principles and the narrowing of the areas of difference
in practice.[36]

The author of *ARS No. 7* added to the controversy with his contention that diversity in accounting among independent entities is
a basic fact of life and thus a basic concept of accounting.[37] But
crime and poverty, too, can be readily justified if all that is required
is to show that they exist. The real question is whether diversity
should exist.[38] The issue remains unresolved for a number of reasons, including (1) failure to identify the real issues, (2) semantic
problems, (3) failure to state objectives, (4) disagreement on approach, and (5) lack of knowledge of economic flows.

The Real Issues

Many of the arguments in this controversy are highly emotional.
It is contended, for example, that uniformity will destroy the
accountant's professional status and initiative and reduce him to
the status of a clerk applying a rule book. In opposition it is contended that the accountant's professional status is being attacked
since it is believed that he willingly aids management in selecting
alternatives that will produce a biased report.[39] Unfortunately,
these arguments tend to obscure the real issues: Is any meaningful
uniformity feasible? (2) Is uniformity needed? (3) If so, what
approach should be employed to obtain it?

IS UNIFORMITY FEASIBLE? Some accountants, while supporting
comparability in principle, question that any reasonable degree
of uniformity is feasible, since business entities differ so much. They
have different capabilities, philosophies, business policies, organi-

---

[35] See the first reference cited in footnote 22 above; for an annotated bibliography
on this issue, see Alfred Rappaport, "Seminar Research on Uniformity," *The Accounting Review,* Vol. 40 (July 1965), pp. 646–648.

[36] See Chapter 2, pp. 32–36, for historical background.

[37] Grady, *op. cit.,* pp. 32–35; 379–385.

[38] For further critical discussion, see Chambers, *op. cit.,* pp. 454–456.

[39] Robert M. Trueblood, "Accounting Principles: The Board and Its Problems,"
Empirical Research in Accounting: Selected Studies, 1966, op. cit., p. 186.

zational structures, environments, objectives, future growth considerations, and operations. Regrettably, no convincing factual examples are presented to show why the accounting should differ because, as Grady argues, "judgments and estimates" and "diffusion in decision-making" are involved.[40]

Uniformists are not convinced that comparability in financial information between entities requires "a basic identicalness" in financial or physical conditions or in management policies.[41] Financial statements are or should be descriptions in words and numbers of economic activity and resources. Accounting principles and practices should not differ simply because an entity has, for example, a centralized rather than a decentralized organizational structure or because it produces and sells steel rather than plastic.[42] But, as discussed below, diversity is apparently justified where economic flow patterns differ.

IS UNIFORMITY NEEDED?   The need for uniformity is also questioned by those who believe that consistency or disclosure or both will suffice. Reasonably comparable information will often emerge, or so it is contended, even between two entities from the consistent application of different accounting practices. For example, the periodic charge to operations, except for the start-up period and for periods of marked change in the level of expenditures, is likely to be approximately the same whether research expenditures are expensed as incurred or capitalized and amortized.[43]

But it should be obvious that the exception may in some instances be significant. And, if the policy of immediate expensing does result in periodic charges similar to those obtained under the alternative, it does so in a somewhat accidental manner and leaves the door

[40] Grady, *op. cit.*, p. 34. For additional support of the Grady position and for disagreement that greater comparability is desirable, see D. E. Browne, "Conflicting Objectives and the Necessity of Tradeoff," *Berkeley Symposium on the Foundations of Financial Accounting* (Berkeley, Calif.: Schools of Business Administration, University of California, 1967), pp. 55–66.

[41] John K. Simmonds, "A Concept of Comparability in Financial Reporting," *The Accounting Review*, Vol. 42 (October 1967), p. 692.

[42] Raymond J. Chambers, *Accounting, Evaluation and Economic Behavior* (Englewood Cliffs, N.J.: Prentice-Hall, Inc., 1966), pp. 152–154, 279.

[43] Savoie, *op. cit.*, p. 159. For a computer-based simulation model offering support to this contention, see Andrew M. McCosh, "Accounting Consistency—Key to Stockholder Information," *The Accounting Review*, Vol. 42 (October 1967), pp. 693–700.

open to income manipulation by varying the amount of the expenditures — a question of objectives.

Additional disclosure, along the lines recommended in 1932 to the New York Stock Exchange by an Institute committee, is also supported as a substitute for uniformity.[44] An entity is to be free to choose those broad principles and practices it considers appropriate, but it must disclose them. The Container Corporation of America, for one, includes in its annual report a list of certain accounting principles it follows. For example, inventories are valued at the lower of cost or market, research and development expenditures are expensed as incurred, and land and buildings, and the leases under which they are acquired, are recorded in asset and liability accounts.[45]

This approach suffers from many limitations in addition to the major obstacle of securing agreement on undefined broad principles. In view of the many alternatives available, vast amounts of additional information may have to be disclosed. And the disclosure may be of little utility unless the dollar effects of the alternatives are also revealed. Such information is usually not readily available and may not be accumulated economically. Even if such information were disclosed, the reader may not be competent enough to use it to introduce greater comparability. Finally, substitution of additional disclosure for uniformity may serve only to accentuate a tendency already in existence, namely, that of relying upon disclosure to avoid the task of finding a solution to a difficult problem.

The issue of how to secure uniformity, assuming it is desirable, is discussed separately below.

Semantic Problems

Even if comparability will follow automatically from uniformity, what is meant by uniformity? Uniformity of principles, practices, procedures, broad principles, or concepts? These terms are used so indiscriminately that accountants may not even be debating the same issue.[46]

THE MEANING OF PRINCIPLES. Most of the semantic problems center around the term principles. Spacek, for example, uses it in

---

[44] Carl M. Blumenschein, "Public Confirmation of Accounting Principles," *Financial Executive*, Vol. 35 (March 1967), p. 20.

[45] *Ibid.*, p. 23.

[46] Keller, *op. cit.*, p. 649.

the sense of detailed guides to the accountant's daily work. He espouses the notion that there is one correct way of accounting for an event or a transaction.[47] Adequate disclosure, conservatism, and materiality are, on the other hand, principles to Peloubet.[48] Powell concurs, without defining them, that agreement on broad principles would be desirable.[49]

Acceptance of materiality, conservatism, and disclosure, or the 32 principles in *ARS No. 7* as the broad principles of accounting would not bring about any substantially greater degree of uniformity. None of the practices currently considered unnecessarily diverse would be prohibited. Under such principles, detailed procedures would have to be specified to achieve uniformity.[50] "Procedures" is used here in the Spacek sense of principles — a position consistent with Blough's contention that there is no difference between accounting principles and procedures.[51]

Some clarification of issues would undoubtedly result if the terms used were defined. It might then be possible to determine if a supporter of uniformity were advocating, for example, the straight-line method of computing depreciation charges for all entities. But it seems unlikely that the semantic problems will be resolved until accounting principles are specified clearly. This is no easy task; since its inception, the APB has sought and failed to provide a statement of basic concepts.[52] This failure and the failure to agree on the principles of accounting are due, at least in part, to a failure to specify objectives.

The Need to State Objectives

The failure of the profession to specify the objectives sought when financial statements are presented is a major obstacle to prog-

[47] Leonard Spacek, "Are Accounting Principles Generally Accepted?" *The Journal of Accountancy,* Vol. 111 (April 1961), pp. 41–46. General support of the notion that principles direct action is also found in Robert E. Witschey, "The Business Need for Better Accounting Principles," *The Journal of Accountancy,* Vol. 117 (January 1964), pp. 27–31.

[48] Maurice E. Peloubet, "Is Further Uniformity Desirable or Possible?" *The Journal of Accountancy,* Vol. 111 (April 1961), pp. 35–41.

[49] Weldon Powell, "Putting Uniformity in Financial Accounting into Perspective," *Law and Contemporary Problems,* Vol. 30 (Autumn 1965), pp. 674–689.

[50] Herbert E. Miller, "After There Is Agreement on Broad Accounting Principles — What Then?" *Texas Certified Public Accountant,* Vol. 34 (September 1961), p. 3.

[51] Carman G. Blough, "Principles and Procedures," *The Journal of Accountancy,* Vol. 111 (April 1961), pp. 51–53.

[52] Trueblood, *op. cit.,* p. 188.

ress in the development of accounting theory and practice. It is also a barrier to the resolution of the uniformity issue.

VARIETY IN OBJECTIVES. Do financial statements represent simply an historical reporting to stockholders of management's stewardship of resources entrusted to it? Or are the statements economic assessments of an entity's financial position and results of operations? Are the financial statements presented to stockholders also designed to fulfill the entity's largely undefined reporting responsibility to debtors, labor, consumers, creditors, government, and the public? Certainly, questions may be raised regarding the probability of fulfilling adequately all of these responsibilities with a set of general-purpose statements.

CONFLICTING OBJECTIVES. What if management seeks to conceal information stockholders would prefer to have disclosed? For example, certain managements have attempted to smooth the trend of reported earnings by varying the amount of dividends received and gains and losses recognized on sales of securities of nonconsolidated subsidiaries.[53] Should the principles of accounting be formulated so that the accountant could condemn this action as manipulation? Or should the principles sanction this action as good income management?[54]

Until agreement is reached on objectives, any attempt to state principles or to evaluate the utility of any particular principle or procedure seems "truly an exercise in futility."[55]

Disagreement on Approach

Despite agreement on the desirability of comparability and the need to restrict the number of alternatives in accounting, there is sharp disagreement about how to attain these goals. Basically, two approaches are advocated: authoritative prescription and acceptance in practice. Some differences of opinion may be found among supporters of each approach. For example, advocates of prescription include (1) those who believe the APB should promulgate a set of accounting principles, (2) those who favor an accounting

[53] Dopuch and Drake, *op. cit.,* pp. 192–207.

[54] Leonard M. Savoie, "Discussion of the Effect of Alternative Accounting Rules for Nonsubsidiary Investments," *Empirical Research in Accounting: Selected Studies, 1966, op. cit.,* p. 226.

[55] Rappaport, *op. cit.,* p. 644.

court,[56] and (3) those who advocate a commission to determine accounting principles, leaving selection of principles in a given instance to the certified public accountant.[57] On the other hand, some advocates of the test of acceptance in practice believe the APB can help to weed out some undesirable or obsolete practices.

AUTHORITATIVE PRESCRIPTION. Opponents of uniformity and prescription contend that uniformists seek to deny management one of its prerogatives—the authority to choose the accounting principles it considers appropriate. And some have recommended that management should not be allowed to control the contents of financial reports. Doubt exists that effective communication or an unbiased reporting can follow if "the player controls the score."[58] Such control is to be placed in the hands of the certified public accountant, individually or collectively.

LIMITATIONS AND IMPLICATIONS. This approach is of doubtful efficacy as long as accounting principles are not authoritatively detailed. Management, by continuing to pay the accountant's fee, retains the ability to exert pressure on the accountant to accept its views. And if principles are not authoritatively detailed, it may be able to switch to auditors who are in agreement with its position or views.

Opponents of prescription are quick to point out that management may be held legally responsible to stockholders for damages suffered from false and misleading financial statements. They question whether management can be held responsible and accountable to stockholders if it is deprived of its authority to choose the principles and practices it considers appropriate in fulfilling its responsibilities.[59] Such a shift in authority may well be accompanied by an increase in the accountant's legal responsibility to his client, to stockholders, and to other interested parties. To a profession seriously questioning

[56] Leonard Spacek, "The Need for an Accounting Court," *The Accounting Review*, Vol. 33 (July 1958), pp. 368–379.

[57] Briloff, *op. cit.*, pp. 81–84, Chap. 5.

[58] Herbert E. Miller, "Audited Statements—Are They Really Management's?" *The Journal of Accountancy*, Vol. 118 (October 1964), p. 44. See also Charles E. Johnson, "Management's Role in External Accounting Measurements," *Research in Accounting Measurement, op. cit.*, pp. 88–100.

[59] Herman W. Bevis, *Corporate Financial Reporting in a Competitive Economy* (New York: The Macmillan Company, 1965), p. 185.

whether it can survive under its existing legal burden, such a shift of responsibility would hardly be welcomed.[60]

Opponents of prescription also question the Board's authority to enforce adherence to uniform accounting principles. The Board has only the power to require members of the Institute to disclose deviations from Board pronouncements. And there are indications that some clients will refuse to follow Board pronouncements — as they did the Board's proposed opinion on accounting for income taxes.[61] Should deviations from Board pronouncements come to be regarded of little consequence, the prestige and respect commanded by the Board, the AICPA, and the individual CPA may be seriously damaged.

THE ALTERNATIVE.   Opponents of prescription contend that alternatives will always exist in accounting as principles and practices are developed to meet the new problems created by an ever changing society. Eventually the number of alternatives may be narrowed as a particular one is clearly established through use as superior. But progress is better served by an evolutionary process involving the interplay of diverse judgments than through decisions of a centralized authority.[62] Any hasty, ill-conceived attempt to accelerate this evolutionary process by authoritative prescription could have a calamitous effect if the prescriptions cause deviations from the evolving trend.

But the current criticism is not that accounting has failed to respond to change. Rather, it does not have a means of weeding out undesirable principles and practices. The result is that a form of Gresham's law is in operation — bad principles and practices are driving out the good. The Board has had some success in eliminating undesirable practices — for example, pay-as-you-go accounting for pensions. It has yet to demonstrate that it can resolve any of the major issues in any manner other than accepting the alternatives now existing in practice.

---

[60] For brief summaries of some of these actions, see Briloff, *op. cit.*, pp. 140–145. The AICPA has also sought the advice of the chief counsel of the SEC regarding a proposed Institute effort to amend the Securities Act of 1933 to limit the accountant's liability under that act; *The CPA*, Vol. 47 (October 1967), p. 1.

[61] "Survey of Current Practices in Accounting for Investment Tax Credit and in Allocating Income Taxes," *op. cit.*, p. 88.

[62] Savoie, "Accounting Improvement: How Fast, How Far?" *op. cit.*, pp. 149–150.

COLLECTIVE RESPONSIBILITY.   While a management may seek to differentiate its product or its research, production, and marketing activities in quest of competitive advantage, it does not follow that accounting principles and practices should be similarly differentiated for competitive reasons. Society as a whole seeks an optimal allocation of resources, and this in turn depends upon the reliability and comparability of financial information. Accounting principles are, for this reason, tinged with a public interest and must be the collective responsibility of the profession.[63] The logical first step in fulfilling this responsibility would be the Board's promulgation of a set of accounting principles.

Lack of Knowledge of Economic Flows

The assumption that comparability will follow automatically from uniformity has already been noted. But comparability is not achieved when dissimilar economic circumstances are made to appear similar. Comparability has the twin objectives of making similarities appear similar and differences different.[64]

UNIFORM VARIABLES.   Many variables must be dealt with in financial reporting, and uniformity in most of them is a prerequisite to comparability. Uniformity or standardization in terminology is an obvious must.[65] This extends to all of the terms used in financial statements, including those in the footnotes. Comparable reporting of an economic event also requires the use of the same basis of valuation and unit of measure.[66]

As noted, considerable evidence exists that, given an environment of substantial inflation, the accounting profession will seek to provide price-level adjusted information. Substantial standardization in terminology also seems attainable. But agreement on the basis of valuation is another matter and is not likely to be secured until agreement is reached on objectives. Practical considerations — acceptability for tax purposes and ease of implementation — seem likely to play an important role here.

---

[63]George C. Mead, "Professional Responsibility in Reporting," *The Journal of Accountancy,* Vol. 117 (January 1964), pp. 37–43.

[64]Simmonds, *op. cit.,* p. 692.

[65]Committee to Prepare a Statement of Basic Accounting Theory, *A Statement of Basic Accounting Theory* (Evanston, Ill.: American Accounting Association, 1966), p. 13.

[66]Simmonds, *op. cit.,* pp. 683–685. See also Martin O. Jager, "Purposes and Possibilities of Uniform Accounting," *Australian Accountant,* Vol. 29 (April 1959), pp. 182–185.

PERIODIC ASSIGNMENTS. Probably the most difficult problems encountered in financial accounting attend the assignment of costs and revenues to periods. And since accounting is to report upon economic activity, these assignments ideally should reflect as closely as possible the flows of economic resources — service potential — that constitute this activity.

Unfortunately, no available devices yield unquestioned measurements of the growth or expiration of service potential. Even market values are questioned. The difficulties encountered in measuring these flows are often so great as to leave the impression that this objective is typically ignored in practice.[67] Attention is directed rather toward ensuring that accounting assignments are systematic and rational and not unduly difficult to implement. Yet resolution of some of the many difficult problems in accounting — choice of inventory or depreciation methods, tax allocation, leases, etc. — would seem to depend, in part, upon securing knowledge of the actual flow of economic benefits.

This lack of knowledge tends to support the notion of uniformity in accounting practices within industries. If actual flow patterns are unknown, won't more comparable and hence more useful information result from applying uniform rather than diverse practices? Isn't this the best that can be achieved under these conditions? And it would seem that, if it were not for the impediments to the mobility of capital, knowledge, and labor in imperfect markets, the flow patterns of firms in an industry might be somewhat similar.

But because these impediments do exist, the probability that flow patterns may differ must be recognized. If so, accounting measurements of these patterns must differ. These are the underlying circumstances which justify alternatives. Comparability will not follow from a uniform accounting treatment of differing economic flow patterns. Supporters of uniformity must recognize that "comparability is the constant and uniformity the variant, applicable where justified by similar economic flows and not applicable where economic flows are dissimilar."[68]

Ascertaining the pattern of expiration of the service potential in many types of assets — tangible and intangible, depreciable and amortizable — is very difficult. It will undoubtedly involve the question of what constitutes reasonable evidence and rejection of the idea that only vouchers supported by canceled checks and in-

[67]Johnson, *op. cit.,* p. 91.
[68]Simmonds, *op. cit.,* p. 692.

voices possess the required degree of verifiability. In some instances, physical flows may provide a clue to economic flows. While in a cost-based accounting system there may be merit in assigning costs to periods according to the physical flow of things, cost assignments not supported by measurements of economic or physical flows will of necessity remain somewhat arbitrary. Hopefully, research aimed at identifying the basic economic flows and at developing new and improved measurement techniques will provide the knowledge sought.[69]

Comparability and Relevance

That the comparability of information will increase its utility is unquestioned. The accountant should, for this reason, strive to present information having the optimal amount of comparability — that is, with consideration given to the cost of accumulating it. But he must recognize clearly that he may not have provided the most useful information possible even though that presented possesses a high degree of comparability. The primary attribute of useful information is relevance.[70] Other attributes, such as verifiability, quantifiability, and freedom from bias, also affect the utility of information and may play an important role in determining what information is actually presented. But information is useless if it is not relevant. For this reason, the accountant must seek to determine what information is truly relevant to users.

The accounting profession must respond to the demands currently placed upon it if it is to remain a viable and vital element in our society. And respond it will. But it seems unlikely that the maturing profession, as evidenced by the increased emphasis upon research, will allow its response to be shaped in the unstructured, *ad hoc* manner of the past.

SUMMARY

The APB found the principles presented in *ARS No. 3* so radically different from present generally accepted accounting principles that the study could not serve as a basis for a Board pronouncement.

---

[69] For an example of one such research effort, see Kristian S. Palda, *The Measurement of Cumulative Advertising Effects,* (Englewood Cliffs, N.J.: Prentice-Hall, Inc., 1964).

[70] *A Statement of Basic Accounting Theory, op. cit.,* p. 9.

The *ARS No. 3* principles differed radically in their general emphasis upon value and replacement cost rather than historical cost as a basis of asset valuation and in their rejection of the cost-attach and realization principles of accounting.

Subsequently, *ARS No. 7* was submitted to the Board not as a statement of what accounting principles should be (although its author did attempt some justification of the principles presented) but as an inventory of present generally accepted accounting principles and their methods of application. There is too much support in the literature and in accounting practice to deny that the inventory is not relatively complete and accurate. But in view of the vast array of alternatives considered acceptable and the fact that the principles presented are often contradictory, the crucial issue is whether they should be the principles of accounting.

Uniformity reappeared as a controversial issue partly because some feared that the Board would prescribe a set of uniform principles and require rigid adherence to them. Also, because accountants tended to air their differences publicly, users of financial information became more acutely aware that accounting alternatives could and did bring about a lack of comparability. The result was a strong demand for greater uniformity in the expectation that uniformity would result in comparability.

Uniformity remains an unresolved issue for a number of reasons. Some question whether it is needed if different practices are consistently applied and disclosed; others doubt that it is feasible in view of the diversity in business. Semantic problems abound to such an extent that effective communication is difficult. Since there is no real agreement on the objectives of accounting, the utility of various principles and practices cannot be readily evaluated. Disagreement exists on approach, with some favoring authoritative prescription of principles while others prefer to let them evolve out of practice. And, finally, lack of knowledge of the actual flow of economic resources (service potential) gives rise to alternatives, such as the two acceptable methods of accounting for the investment tax credit.

While comparability in financial reporting does require uniformity in many of the reporting variables — terminology, basis of valuation, unit of measure — it does not require the complete elimination of alternatives. Alternatives are needed to ensure comparable reflection of differing economic flow patterns, such as the rates of expiration of service potential in differing assets.

But in the search for comparability the accountant must never forget that, basically, relevance gives information utility. While quantification, verifiability, and freedom from bias tend to add to the utility of information, irrelevant information is useless.

QUESTIONS

1. (a) Outline how the Accounting Principles Board has responded to the charge of providing statements of basic postulates and accounting principles. (b) Evaluate this response.

2. (a) Summarize the major recommendations (principles) presented in *ARS No. 3*. (b) Are these recommendations "too radically different" from currently accepted practices? Explain.

3. *ARS No. 3* recommended that amounts payable in the future be discounted to obtain their present values and that such values be recorded. Is this truly a "radical" departure from present practice? Explain.

4. (a) Contrast carefully the approaches followed by the authors of *ARS No. 3* and *ARS No. 7*. (b) What is the natural result of this difference in approach?

5. Present three examples to show that the principles in *ARS No. 7* fail to provide the guidance expected from principles.

6. It is alleged that Principle C-2 in *ARS No. 7* is of no value since it provides no guidance at all — assets are to be valued at cost or not at cost. Explain how this same argument can be applied to another principle in that study.

7. Does the use of a "Reserve for Self-Insurance" violate Principle A-5 of *ARS No. 7*? Explain.

8. Present an over-all evaluation of the principles contained in *ARS No.7*.

9. Which of the principles presented in *ARS No. 7* are no longer to be considered generally accepted because of subsequent action by the Accounting Principles Board?

10. (a) What is meant by "weasel word"? (b) Give several examples of weasel words used in accounting. (c) Explain carefully, by illustration, why one of your examples is a weasel word.

11. Do you believe that financial statements (as conventionally prepared and presented) are fair *and* in accord with generally accepted accounting principles, fair *because* they are in accord with these principles, or fair *only to the extent* that these principles are fair? Explain.

12. Why are there so many alternatives in accounting? Explain and illustrate.

13. It has been suggested that, as a substitute for uniformity in practices, an entity be allowed to choose the broad principles of accounting it considers applicable but that it be required to disclose the principles chosen. How feasible and adequate a substitute is this for uniformity?

14. Present three examples of practices which, if employed, would lead to conflicting objectives.

15. Outline briefly the history of the uniformity issue in accounting and give reasons why the issue apparently attracted greater attention at certain times than at others.

16. (a) What, in general, has been the response of users of financial information to the employment of accounting alternatives? (b) How have financial analysts attempted to take them into consideration in their analyses? (c) What are the limitations in this approach?

17. Evaluate the contention that consistency in the application of different accounting principles by individual entities will yield comparable information between entities.

18. How might it be argued that differences in management philosophy can and *should* lead to differences in accounting? Explain carefully.

19. Will uniformity in accounting principles bring about the desired comparability in financial information? Explain.

20. What are the implications of the contrast between the basic concept in *ARS No. 7* of "Diversity in Accounting among Independent Entities" and the following quotation from the charter of the APB: "The general purpose of the Institute . . . should be to advance the written expression of what constitutes generally accepted accounting principles. . . . It means continuing effort to determine appropriate practice and to narrow the areas of difference and inconsistency in practice"?

21. Is there only one valid accounting interpretation of an economic event? Or must the interpretation always take into consideration other factors, such as the environment, with the result that alternative interpretations are always possible? Explain.

22. What are the major advantages and disadvantages of the authoritative prescription approach of determining accounting principles and of eliminating alternatives in the quest for comparable financial information?

23. Does the history of accounting suggest that preferred accounting principles and practices survive while undesirable ones die? Explain.

24. What, in your opinion, is the greatest obstacle to obtaining comparable financial information? Explain.

25. How can it be argued that dangers lie in devoting too much attention to the issue of uniformity in accounting and toward the need for comparable financial information? Explain.

26. In your opinion, how will the accounting profession resolve many of the issues and problems it now faces? Do you believe this is the way they should be resolved? Explain.

INDEX

Absorption costing, 115
Accounting alternatives, 131–136
Accounting income, 75–94
  and changing price levels, 78–88
  current cost, 88–90
  income inclusions and exclusions,
    90–94
  all-inclusive concept, 90–91
  current operating performance
    concept, 91–92
  transactions approach, 76–78
Accounting principles, 46ff., 123ff.
Accounting Research Bulletins of
  AICPA, 2, 34–35
Accounting Research Studies of
  AICPA, 35–36
Accounting theory
  approaches, 2–13
    axiomatic, 12
    behavioral, 13
    communication theory, 12
    deductive, 5–8, 36, 46
    ethical, 10–12
    inductive, 8–10
    practical, 2–5
    sociological, 13
  attributes, 16–17
  basic concepts, 46–66
    conservatism, 57–58
    consistency, 55–56
    continuity, 51–53
    dependability of data, 58–61
    diversity, 56
    going concern, 51–53
    materiality, 61–62
    monetary expression in accounts,
      53–55
    nature of, 47–48
    society and government structure
      honoring private-property rights,
      48–49
    specific business entities, 49–51
    timeliness, 63–64
  defined, 1
  sources of, 20–43
    environmental influences, 20–32
    organizational influences, 32–43
  uses
    directive, 15–16
    nondirective, 14–15

Accretion processes and revenue
  recognition, 107
All-inclusive concept, 73, 82, 90–91
American Accounting Association,
  36–39
  Committee on Accounting Concepts
    and Standards, 27, 88, 98, 100,
    102, 109, 110
  Committee to Prepare a Statement
    of Basic Accounting Theory, 1,
    47, 73, 88, 99, 144, 146
  Concepts and Standards Research
    Study Committee, 50, 51, 101,
    103, 104, 108, 114, 117, 118
  influence on theory, 36–39
  Monograph No. 3, 39, 47ff., 98,
    101, 105, 111, 116
  1936 statement and revisions,
    37–38, 46ff., 69, 88, 98, 99, 100,
    102, 109, 110
  1966 statement, 1, 14, 38–39, 47ff.,
    69, 73, 86, 88, 99, 144, 146
American Institute of Certified Public
  Accountants, 32–36
  Accounting Principles Board, 35,
    78, 140ff.
    Opinion No. 1, 36
    Opinion No. 2, 36, 61
    Opinion No. 3, 35
    Opinion No. 4, 36
    Opinion No. 5, 26, 35
    Opinion No. 6, 28, 36, 43
    Opinion No. 7, 35
    Opinion No. 8, 32, 35, 132
    Opinion No. 9, 36, 62, 63, 92–94,
      99, 118
    Opinion No. 10, 36, 106
    Opinion No. 11, 35, 49, 114, 132
    Opinion No. 12, 36
  Accounting Research Bulletins, 2,
    32, 34–35, 109, 125
    No. 1, 34
    No. 43, 34, 35, 92
    No. 51, 2, 34, 61
  Accounting Research Studies, 35–36
    No. 1, 7, 8, 10, 11, 12, 15, 27, 35,
      36, 46ff., 124
    No. 2, 35
    No. 3, 6, 7, 35, 36, 98, 100, 104,
      108, 109, 123–125, 146–147

American Institute of Certified Public
    Accountants (continued)
    No. 4, 35
    No. 5, 26, 35
    No. 6, 30, 35, 78, 83, 85, 86, 87,
        90
    No. 7, 3, 11, 31, 35, 36, 46ff., 98,
        105, 106, 125–131, 133, 137,
        138, 140, 147
    No. 8, 31, 32, 35
    No. 9, 35
    Accounting Terminology Bulletins,
        34, 109, 110
    Committees on Accounting
        Procedure and Terminology,
        2, 29, 30, 34
    Committee on Auditing Procedure,
        12
    cooperation with NYSE, 33–34
    influence on theory, 32–36
    Terminology Bulletin 1, 34
    "Uniform Accounting," 32–33
Asset costs
    donated, 113
    group purchase, 113
    self-constructed, 113–114
Asset valuation, 24
    cost, 42
Assets defined, 109–110
Axiomatic approach, 12
Behavioral approach, 13
Bias, 38, 58, 59, 73, 146
Bond discount, 28
Capital
    maintenance, 27, 28, 76–77
    money investment concept, 77–78
Capitalized net receipts, 71–74
Cash collection basis of revenue
    recognition, 105–106
Cash discounts, 100
Cash flows, 73
Collection costs, 116
Communication theory approach, 12
Comparability, 137–138, 146
Conglomerates, 32, 41
Conservatism concept, 57–58
Consistency concept, 55–56
Consolidated statements, 23, 34
Continuity concept, 51–53
Cost accounting, 32
Cost or market, whichever is lower,
    3, 33, 57
Cost-recovery approach to revenue
    recognition, 106
Costs
    period, 116–118
    direct, nonproduct, 115
    product, 115
Critical event theory, 104–105, 106,
    107
Current cost, 88–90
Current cost in statements, 39

Current cost or value, 111–112
Current operating performance
    concept, 91–92
Deductive approach, 5–8, 36, 46
Dependability of data concept, 58–61
Depreciation accounting, 24
    accelerated methods, 25, 26, 30, 112
Direct costing, 27, 115
Discount on debt, 28
Discounting receivables and payables,
    99–100
Discounts on sales, 100
Diversity concept, 56
Diversity vs. uniformity, 136–146
Divisional reporting, 39, 41
Donated asset cost, 113
Double-entry bookkeeping, 6, 20–21
Earning process, 101–102
Economic conditions, influence on
    theory, 29–32
Economic income, 70–74
Economic theory as influence on
    accounting theory, 27
Enterprise theory, 23
Entity concept, 37, 49–51
Entity theory, 23
Ethical approach, 10–12
Expenses
    defined, 109–111
    measurement, 111–114
    recognition, 109–119
    time, 114–118
Expenses and revenues, 97–119
Federal Power Commission regulations,
    28–29, 32
Federal Trade Commission, 42
Financial Executives Institute, 41
Financial statement objectives, 141
Financial statement standardization,
    32–33
Financial statements, modern form, 24
Freedom from bias, 38, 59, 146
Gains and losses on monetary items,
    84–86
Going-concern concept, 22, 51–53
Historical cost, 5, 39, 42, 53, 112–114
Income concepts, 69–94
    accounting income, 75–94
        and changing price levels, 78–88
        current cost, 88–90
        income inclusions and exclusions,
            90–94
        transactions approach, 76–78
    economic income, 70–74
        capitalized net receipts, 71–74
        market values, 74–75
    psychic income, 70
Income determination, 69–70, 97
    balance sheet approach, 80–82
    transactions approach, 82–83
Income maintenance, 27
Income taxes, nature of, 110

Index number problem, 87–88
Inductive approach, 8–10
Installment basis of revenue
    recognition, 106
Installment sales, 26, 42–43
Interest, 29
Interest, nature of, 110
Internal control, 58–61
Interstate Commerce Commission,
    classification of accounts, 28
Inventory valuation
    last-in, first-out, 26, 30, 57, 112
    lower of cost or market, 3, 33, 57
Liquidation value, 52, 75
Long-term leases, disclosure, 11, 26
Losses, 118
    defined, 109
Losses and gains on monetary items,
    84–86
Lower of cost or market, 3, 33
Market values, 74–75
Matching, 114
Materiality concept, 61–62
Monetary concept, 30, 53–55
Monetary gains and losses, 84–86
Monetary item adjustment, 81–82
Money investment concept of capital,
    77–78
New York Stock Exchange cooperation
    with AICPA, 33–34
Nonmonetary item adjustment, 81
Objectives, 5
Objectivity, 59
Pension movement, effect of on accounting
    theory, 31–33
Pensions, accounting for, 5, 31–32, 132
Percentage-of-completion basis of revenue
    recognition, 106–107
Periodic assignment of costs and revenues,
    145–146
Physical capacity maintenance, 89–90
Pooling-of-interests, 25, 26, 28–29, 32
Postulates, 5, 123, 124
Practical approach, 2–5
Price-level-adjusted data, effect on ratios,
    86–87
Price-level-adjustment ratio, 81
Price-level changes, 30–31, 39, 78–88
Price-level index number problem, 87–88
Principles, 5, 46ff., 123ff.
Private-property rights, basic concept, 48–49
Product costs, 115
Production bases of revenue recognition,
    106–108
Proprietary theory, 23
Psychic income, 70
Public utility regulation, 28–29
Purchasing power concept, 78–79

Quantifiability, 38, 146
Quasi-reorganizations, 30
Railroad regulation, 28
Realizable gain, 89
Realization, 27, 37, 66, 75, 77, 85–86,
    102–104, 105, 114
Realized income, 73
Relevance, 38, 146
Replacement prices, 75, 112
Research and development expenditures, 26
Residual equity theory, 23
Revenue
    defined, 98–99
    measurement, 99–100
    recognition, 97–109
        bases, 105–108
        time, 100–105
Revenue modifications, 110
Revenue realization, 27, 102–104
Revenues and expenses, 97–119
Rules, 6
Sales basis of revenue recognition, 105
Securities and Exchange Commission,
    29–30, 39–43, 132
    Accounting Series Releases, 40
    Accounting Series Release No. 4, 40–41
    Accounting Series Releases, 29–30, 40, 41
    influence on theory, 39–43
    Regulation S-X, 40, 41
Self-constructed asset cost, 113–114
Service potentials, 109
Social conditions, influence on theory,
    29–32
Sociological approach, 13
Stable dollar assumption, 54
Stewardship, 113
Stock dividends, 25, 26
Stock option plans, 25
Study Group on Business Income,
    31, 66
Subjective income, 72ff.
Tax allocation, 132
Taxation as influence on accounting
    theory, 25–27
Timeliness concept, 63–64
Transactions approach, 76–78
Treasury stock, 25, 34, 37
Uncollectible accounts receivable, 100
"Uniform Accounting" and revisions,
    32–33
Uniformity vs. diversity, 136–146
Unrealized income, 73, 85
Uses of accounting theory, 14–16
Verifiability, 38, 146
Warranty costs, 116
Weasel words, 131
Wisc   Public Service Commission,
    28